TURY

FICTION AND NON-FICTION

EDITED BY
CHRISTOPHER EDGE

OXFORD
UNIVERSITY PRESS

OXFORD

UNIVERSITY PRESS

Great Clarendon Street, Oxford, OX2 6DP,
United Kingdom

Oxford University Press is a department of the University of Oxford.
It furthers the University's objective of excellence in research, scholarship,
and education by publishing worldwide. Oxford is a registered trade mark
of Oxford University Press in the UK and in certain other countries

British Library Cataloguing in Publication Data

Data available

ISBN 978-0-19-836790-1

3 5 7 9 10 8 6 4 2

Printed in Italy by L.E.G.O SpA

Contents

War and disaster

Introduction

The 20th and 21st centuries have been an era of immense change. The first decade of the 20th century saw the Wright brothers make the first powered human flight in a flimsy aircraft called the Flyer, which stayed aloft for only a few seconds, while today astronauts orbit the Earth for months at a time in the International Space Station.

During this time, the planet has been scarred by two World Wars and countless disasters, both natural and man-made, but has also seen some of humanity's greatest achievements. Advances in science and technology have transformed our understanding of the world and our place in the universe, and helped us to witness momentous events and changes in society.

In this collection you will read fiction, non-fiction and literary non-fiction from every decade of the 20th century and the 21st to date, organised into themes that help you to explore different aspects of life during this period. There are extracts from novels and short stories by authors such as Graham Greene, Roald Dahl, Beryl Bainbridge and Margaret Atwood, and an array of non-fiction and literary non-fiction from authors such as George Orwell and Simon Armitage, including autobiographies and memoirs, newspaper articles and blogs, travel writing, letters, speeches, editorials and transcripts.

The extracts in this collection have been arranged so that the different texts help to illuminate each other, helping you to draw connections between non-fiction and fiction and build a picture of the times in which these texts were first written and read. For example, you will read a letter about the prospect of space exploration published in *The Times* newspaper in 1956, then read an extract from a science-fiction novel by Arthur C. Clarke about the colonization of the moon which was first published in 1961, before reading extracts from Neil Armstrong and Edwin 'Buzz' Aldrin's accounts of the first Moon landing.

This collection can also be used alongside the companion *19th-Century Fiction and Non-fiction* collection as it shares the same thematic organisation.

As George Orwell, one of the writers collected here, once wrote:

"Each generation imagines itself to be more intelligent than the one that went before it, and wiser than the one that comes after it."

I hope by reading the texts in this collection you gain a greater understanding of the lives of previous generations and an appreciation of the achievements of your own.

Christopher Edge

School and childhood

Looking back at life for children in the 20th century can often highlight differences with the lives of 21st-century children today. From the clothes they wore to the way they spent their free time, on the surface obvious contrasts can be seen. However, concerns about the attitudes and behaviour of young people is a constant theme throughout the 20th and 21st centuries and some of the texts in this section defend 'modern youth' against such criticisms.

Another constant is experiences of school life, which has been depicted in both fiction and non-fiction, from difficulties with teachers to the challenge of making new friends. The problems faced by children during this era are also explored, from evacuation during the Second World War to the consequences of divorce.

Letter to *The Times* newspaper about 'Modern Youth'

Concerns about the youth of today aren't just a recent phenomenon, with teenagers in the 1920s finding their attitudes and behaviour criticized in the press. However in this letter from the Archdeacon of Chesterfield, which was published in *The Times* newspaper on 23rd April 1923, modern youth finds an unexpected ally.

Sir,

The criticisms which have appeared in the correspondence on 'Modern Youth' have been on the severe side, though undoubtedly all that has been said must be acknowledged as embodying truth, but there is one aspect of the conduct of young people to which full justice has not been given, and that is the relationship between modern youth and old age. The **graciousness** of present-day youth to old age stands out as a remarkable contrast to the stilted respect of half a century ago. Affection was none the less true and sincere, no doubt, though we always addressed our fathers and **grandsires** as 'Sir,' and always rose when they entered the room where we were; but I do not recall my own relationship with the elders as being what I can speak of as quite natural and at ease.

Today it is much different. A while ago I happened to be present at a point-to-point hunt meeting, the first I had attended since my youth, but I could not help noticing the delightful and friendly way in which the young men and women came and chatted to me and to other old fogeys who were there, talking quite naturally about the events, the horses and the riders and even confiding their '**backings**'. It was very different half a century ago. The same kindliness runs through all classes. On a wild stormy night during the past winter I had occasion on a Sunday night to take the service in an outlying district church two miles from my house. Two young **collier** lads insisted on walking home with me a long distance out of their way 'because it was not fit for an old gentleman to go alone on a night like that,' and they came in the soaking rain, though one of them had to change and go to work that night.

I grant the young people often startle me, and I sometimes wonder! but their kindliness, their openness and their gracious consideration of age make me feel they are the most lovable youth of all time. It is the same with the young children. We are told they are independent and wilful and undisciplined, but there is a wonderful charm in their quite natural absence of 'awe' for the old people. In passing along one of the streets in our mining village, I was hailed and conducted into the backyard of a cottage home, a chair was brought from the cottage, and

3

I witnessed a children's performance – 'Little Red Riding Hood,' a fairy dance, a recitation and several songs. The dresses were made by the children of coloured crinkly paper and various homely devices which included old curtains and door-mats. The yard was full of children as spectators with a few collier lads. It was a priceless show, and had taken most of the Easter week holiday to prepare. There was no shyness and the stage manageress explained to me all details. The matter of note is that a lot of children should care to bring in an old gentleman and seemingly like to have him there just as one of themselves.

With all the difficulties which youth presents in these days (and, my word, they are real difficulties) at least let it be chronicled there never was a time when the young were more gracious to the old.

Yours. &c..

E. F. CROSSE

---

graciousness pleasantness and generosity
grandsires old-fashioned term for grandfathers
backings horses that have been 'backed' or bet on to win
collier coal miner

Extract from *Lord Emsworth and the Girl Friend* by P. G. Wodehouse

FICTION

The following extract is taken from 'Lord Emsworth and the Girl Friend', a short story by P. G. Wodehouse. Here, Lord Emsworth is visiting the annual fete, thrown for the young people of the nearby village, Blandings Parva, in the grounds of his castle. In addition to the local schoolchildren, a group of children from London, who have been sent to experience the fresh air of the countryside, are also visiting the village. In this extract, Lord Emsworth has just stepped inside a marquee at the fete to find the children taking tea there.

Once in the tent, it took his experienced eye but a moment to discern that the present feast was eclipsing in frightfulness all its predecessors.

Young Blandings Parva, in its normal form, tended rather to the stolidly **bovine** than the riotous. In all villages, of course, that must of necessity be an occasional tough egg – in the case of Blandings Parva the names of Willie Drake and Thomas (Rat-Face) Blenkiron spring to the mind – but it was seldom that the local infants offered anything beyond the power of a **curate** to control. What was giving the present gathering its striking resemblance to a reunion of *sans-culottes* at the height of the French Revolution was the **admixture** of the Fresh Air London visitors.

About the London child, reared among the tin cans and cabbage stalks of Drury Lane and Clare Market, there is a breezy **insouciance** which his country cousin lacks. Years of back-chat with annoyed parents and relatives have cured him of any tendency he may have had towards shyness, with the result that when he requires anything he grabs for it, and when he is amused by any slight peculiarity in the personal appearance in members of the governing classes he finds no difficulty in translating his thoughts into speech. Already, up and down the long tables, the curate's unfortunate squint was coming in for hearty comment, and the front teeth of one of the school-teachers ran it a close second for popularity. Lord Emsworth was not, as a rule, a man of swift inspirations, but it occurred to him at this juncture that it would be a prudent move to take off his top hat before his little guests observed it and appreciated its humorous possibilities.

The action was not, however, necessary. Even as he raised his hand a rock cake, singing through the air like a shell, took it off for him.

Lord Emsworth had had sufficient. Even Constance, unreasonable woman though she was, could hardly expect him to stay and beam genially under conditions like this. All civilized laws had obviously gone by the board and Anarchy reigned in the marquee. The curate was doing his best to form a provisional government consisting of himself and the two school-teachers, but there was only one man who could have coped adequately with the situation and that was King Herod who – regrettably – was not among those present. Feeling like some aristocrat of the **old *régime*** sneaking away from the **tumbril**, Lord Emsworth edged to the exit and withdrew.

---

bovine dull and stupid, like cattle
curate member of the clergy who helps a vicar
sans-culottes lower class people in late-18th century France who became revolutionaries to overthrow the aristocracy
admixture mixing in
insouciance casual lack of concern, indifference
old *régime* the aristocratic system of government in France which was ended by the French Revolution in the late 18th century
tumbril an open cart used to carry condemned prisoners to the guillotine during the French Revolution

7

Editorial from *The Independent* newspaper

The following editorial celebrating the achievements of the youth of today was published in *The Independent* newspaper on the 15th August 2015.

We should celebrate the new generation

The *Independent on Sunday* refuses to share the outdated grumbling about the youth of today. Deference has gone, and quite right too.

As the youngest national newspaper in Britain, *The Independent on Sunday* has always been optimistic, and one of the reasons for our hopefulness has been our faith in young people. Too often, the young are portrayed negatively in the media, as a problem or a threat.

We are encouraged, therefore, that the Government's "horizon scanning" group, which looks out for future opportunities and threats, has recognised that many of the stereotypes of the past are out of date. As we report today, the group notes that young people's use of alcohol, tobacco and illegal drugs has fallen substantially, and that teenage pregnancies are less common than they used to be. Crime and suicide are down. The analysis, carried out for Sir Mark Walport, the Government's chief scientific adviser, and Sir Jeremy Heywood, the Cabinet Secretary, attributes the change to two big causes.

One is that today's and yesterday's parents are better at bringing up children. The youth are no longer as desperate to get away from their parents as they used to be and these days often go on holiday with them or even willingly move back in with them after university. The other is the development of the internet and computer technology, which means that young people have more to do and are usually better informed doing it.

Naturally, as the group points out, the digital life carries its own risks. These range from the relatively trivial, such as not getting enough sleep, through to lack of exercise, and to the more serious problems of self-image and status anxiety, including cyber-bullying, eating disorders and self-harm. Yet these should be seen in perspective.

That is not to say that we should be complacent about the problems of the "always-connected" life and of internet "addiction" – although it is fair to say that these afflict many middle-aged and older people too. Parents, politicians and internet companies need to take their responsibilities seriously to work on practical and supportive ways of protecting teenagers and young adults from the dark side of technology – technology which is otherwise an **incalculable boon**.

But let us for once celebrate the contribution that young people make to society generally. As the group says, four-fifths of 16 to 24-year-olds took part in some voluntary charity or community activity in the past year – more than any other age group. These are things "that often go unrecognised in public debate", the group says. Well, this newspaper is trying to change that, with its *Happy List*, which recognises the selfless contribution made by people – of all ages – throughout the country.

We refuse to share the outdated grumbling about the youth of today. Deference has gone, and quite right too. But public spiritedness and good manners are much more important. *The Independent on Sunday* is proud to take the view that today's young people are the best educated, most socially responsible and most promising generation that this country has ever raised.

---

incalculable not able to be calculated
boon something very useful or practical

Newspaper report about the evacuation of children

> At the outset of the Second World War, the government decided to evacuate children from cities to protect them from enemy air raids, sending the children to live in the countryside. In the following newspaper report, published on the 1st September 1939, the journalist, Hilde Marchant, describes the evacuation of children from the London borough of Camden.

It was not until Friday morning, September 1st, that I really took the sharp, agonized breath of war. That day it began, in a slum in London.

The office had told me to cover the evacuation of some of London's schoolchildren. There had been great preparations for the scheme – preparations that raised strong criticism. Evacuation would split the British home, divide child and parent, break that domestic background that was our strength.

I went to a block of working-class flats at the back of Gray's Inn Road and in the early morning saw a tiny, frail, Cockney child walking across to school. The child had a big, brown-paper parcel in her hand and was dragging it along. But as she turned I saw a brown box banging against her thin legs. It bumped up and down at every step, slung by a thin string over her shoulder.

It was Florence Morecambe, an English schoolchild, with a gas mask instead of a satchel over her shoulder.

I went along with Florence to her school. It was a big Council school and the classrooms were filled with children, parcels, gas masks. The desks and blackboards were piled up in a heap in one corridor. They were not going to school for lessons. They were going on a holiday. The children were excited and happy because their parents had told them they were going away to the country. Many of them, like my little Florence, had never seen green fields. Their playground was the tarmac or a sandpit in the concrete square at the back.

I watched the schoolteachers calling out their names and tying luggage labels in their coats, checking their parcels to see there were warm and clean clothes. On the gates of the school were two fat policemen. They were letting the children through but gently asking the parents not to come farther. They might disturb the children. So mothers and fathers were saying goodbye, straightening the girls' hair, getting the boys to blow their noses, and lightly and quickly kissing them. The parents stood outside while the children went to be registered in their classrooms. There was quite a long wait before this small army got its orders through from the LCC [London County Council] to move off. In the meantime I sat in the school playground, watching these thin, wiry little Cockneys playing their rush-and-push games in the faded netball pitch. It was disturbing for through the high grille their mothers pressed their faces, trying to see the one child that resembled them. Every now and then the policeman would call out a child's name and a mother who had forgotten a bar of chocolate or a toothbrush had a last chance to tell a child to be good, to write and to straighten her hat.

Labelled and lined up, the children began to move out of the school. I followed Florence, her live tiny face bobbing about, white among so many navy-blue school caps. She was chattering away to an older schoolgirl, wanting to know what the country was like, where they were going, what games they would play on the grass.

On one side of Gray's Inn Road this ragged crocodile moved towards the tube station. On the other, were mothers who were waving and running along to see the last of their children. The police had asked them not to follow, but they could not resist.

The children scrambled down into the tube.

13

Extract from *Thunder and Lightnings* by Jan Mark

In the following extract from the novel *Thunder and Lightnings* by Jan Mark, first published in 1976, Andrew Mitchell has just started at a new school and has been introduced to a boy named Victor who is working on his school project.

'Miss Beale said you would show me round, to look at the projects,' said Andrew.

'Why, do you want to copy one?' asked Victor, lifting a strand of hair and exposing one eye. 'You could copy mine, only someone might recognize it. I've done that three times already.'

'Whatever for?' asked Andrew. 'Don't you get tired of it?'

Victor shook his head and his hair.

'That's only once a year. I did that two times at the junior school and now I'm doing that again,' he said. 'I do fish, every time. Fish are easy. They're all the same shape.'

'No, they're not,' said Andrew.

'They are when I do them,' said Victor. He spun

his book round, with one finger, to show Andrew the drawings. His fish were not only all the same shape, they were all the same shape as slugs. Underneath each drawing was a printed heading: BRAEM; TENSH; CARP; STIKLBAK; SHARK. It was the only way of telling them apart. The shark and the bream were identical, except that the shark had a row of teeth like tank traps.

'Isn't there a 'c' in stickleback?' said Andrew. Victor looked at his work.

'You're right.' He crossed out both 'k's, substituted 'c's and pushed the book away, the better to study it. 'I got that wrong last year.'

Andrew flipped over a few pages. There were more slugs: PLACE; COD: SAWFISH; and a stringy thing with a frill round its neck: EEL.

'Don't you have to write anything?' asked Andrew.

'Yes, look. I wrote a bit back here. About every four pages will do,' said Victor. 'Miss Beale, she keep saying I ought to write more but she's glad when I don't. She's got to read it. Nobody can read my writing.'

Andrew was not surprised. Victor's writing was a sort of code to deceive the enemy, with punctuation marks in unlikely places to confuse anyone who came too close to cracking the code. He watched Andrew counting the full stops in one sentence and said, 'I put those in while I think about the next word. I like doing question marks better.' He pointed out two or three specimens, independent

15

question marks, without questions. They looked like curled feathers out of a pillow. One had a face.

'Do you put a question mark in every sentence?' said Andrew.

'Oh, yes. I know you don't actually need them,' said Victor, 'but they're nice to do.'

Andrew turned to the last page of the book. There was a drawing of a whale.

'Whales aren't fish,' said Andrew.

'Aren't they?' said Victor. 'Are you sure? I always put a whale in.'

'Whales are mammals.'

'What's a mammal?' said Victor. He wrote 'This. is.not.a.fish?' under his whale and closed the book. 'Come and see the others.'

'Mammals don't lay eggs,' said Andrew, as they set off round the room.

'That's a pity,' said Victor. 'I'd like to see a whale's egg. Big as a bath, wouldn't that be?' He stopped by the boy in the pink shirt. 'Let's have a look at your project, Tim.'

Andrew thought he had seen most of Tim's project before. It featured a man in a tree, knotty with muscles and wearing a leopard skin.

'Tarzan,' said Tim.

'Why do a project about Tarzan?' said Andrew.

'Tarzan's easy,' said Tim. 'You just cut him out and stick him in.'

'Fish are easier,' said Victor.

'Why not do worms then?' said Andrew. 'Nothing could be easier than worms. Wiggle-wiggle-wiggle: all over in a second. Page one, worms are long and thin. Page two, worms are round.'

Victor began to grin but Tim sat down to give the idea serious consideration.

Victor's grin became wider, revealing teeth like Stonehenge.

'I reckon you're catching on,' he said. 'Why don't you do worms?'

'I want to do something interesting,' said Andrew.

'Ho,' said Victor. 'You'll come to a bad end, you will.'

Extract from *Tilly Two Rooms*

The BBC Radio 4 programme *Home Truths* gave ordinary people the chance to share stories about their lives. The following extract is taken from an edition of the programme first broadcast in 2004 and tells the story of Tilly Aldridge, a teenage girl whose parents had divorced. Here, Tilly explains how she spends weekdays at her mother's house and weekends at her father's and so has two very different bedrooms.

'I spend most of my time up here. I love it in my room. You have to have your own space, otherwise you're not comfortable,' Tilly explains. 'If anything's going wrong in the house, you'll always be safe in your room – you always come up here knowing that no one can follow you. I think every teenage girl now goes through the phase where they just don't want to go out of their room because everything is in here that entertains them.'

Tilly describes her room at her mother's house as 'tasteful, modern and comfortable'. The house itself is a vision of gorgeous, white loveliness. Apart, that is, from the fingermarks on the walls . . .

She keeps her room pretty tidy – for a teenager – admitting that when she's in a bad mood and has nothing better to do she'll tidy it up. 'A teenager in a bad mood?' I hear you say. 'That room must be spotless.'

On the subject of moods, it appears that Tilly and her mother, Maddie, have come to a somewhat unusual entente on how Tilly's room is decorated.

'Well, we never argued about it,' Tilly says. 'She chose most of the things that go in here, but I don't mind it at all. It makes me feel a little bit more grown up. Also, my mum picks out things and says, 'This doesn't work,' and so she says, 'Take it over to Dad's house,' and I go on over there and just dump it there.'

Just dump it there – a novel solution. What Tilly dumps are all things that clash with Maddie's white walls and tasteful decor. Posters for a start – unless they're on the specially mounted board. 'If Mum saw the paint coming off the wall then she'd go mad.' And Tilly admits that given half a chance she'd splash around some colour too.

The other thing that Maddie can't stand is stuffed animals. They go straight round to Dad's. However, in the corner of the room there's a doll's house. Not your average, common-or-garden doll's house, but a very modern one: from Bauhaus to doll's house, so to speak. 'Yeah, it's quite different,' Tilly says coolly. 'Sort of adds to the effect that I'm still a child. I don't play with it often.

'When I go round to friends' houses their rooms are

always really messy,' Tilly continues. 'It's a really nice room. I love it, but I know my friends think it's actually quite a boring bedroom.'

A bedroom that Tilly cleans herself. A very different room to the one at her dad's house, because Dad doesn't care one jot what she puts in it, as long as she's happy.

Maddie, it won't surprise you to learn, hopes with a passion that Tilly will take after her: 'I would be absolutely devastated I think if she did do that sort of chintzy, big-sofas, big-curtain thing.'

You might expect a child to dislike commuting between two parents – the transience of it. But Tilly sees only advantages.

'I think I probably prefer it to having one life at one house, because I reckon that's pretty boring. But I've got two houses I can go to, and there's always going to be a charge in the atmosphere between brothers and me and parents, and in the end it's quite nice.

'Sometimes,' she continues, 'I feel like I've been carted from one place to the other. It's not bad that feeling – it's not as bad as everyone thinks having your parents split up. In the end it's sort of for the best, so it doesn't really bother you in the end.'

Extract from *Anita and Me* by Meera Syal

FICTION

> The following extract is taken from the novel *Anita and Me* by Meera Syal, which was first published in 1996. The novel is about Meena Kumar, a nine-year-old girl growing up in the only Punjabi family in the village of Toddington, near Birmingham. Here, Meena describes an encounter with Anita Rutter, another girl from her school.

A shadow fell over my T-bar sandals and I looked up to see Anita Rutter staring at me through squinted eyes ringed in bright blue eyeshadow. She broke off a twig from our privet hedge and thrust it under my nose, pointing at a part of the branch where the leaves were not their usual straight darts but were rolled up in on themselves, neat and packaged as school dinner sandwiches. "See them leaves?" She carefully unrolled one of them: it came away slowly like sticky tape, to reveal a sprinkling of tiny black eggs. "Butterflies' eggs, them is. They roll up the leaf to hid them, see?"

She stripped all the leaves off the twig in one movement and smelled her fingers, before flicking the naked branch at my ankles. It stung but I did not pull my legs back. I knew this was a test.

"What you got?"

I held out my crumpled bag of swollen sweets. She peered inside disdainfully, then snatched the bag off me and began walking away as she ate. I watched her go, confused. I could still hear my parents talking inside, their voices now calmer, conciliatory. Anita stopped momentarily, shouting over her shoulder, "**Yow** coming then?"

It was the first week of the long summer holidays and I had six whole weeks which I could waste or taste. So I got up and followed her without a word.

I was happy to follow her a respectable few paces behind, knowing that I was privileged to be in her company. Anita was the undisputed '**cock' of our yard**, maybe that should have been hen, but her foghorn voice, foul mouth, and proficiency at lassoing victims with her frayed skipping rope indicated she was carrying enough testosterone around to earn the title. She ruled over all the kids in the yard with a mixture of pre-pubescent feminine **wiles**, pouting, sulking, clumsy cack-handed flirting and unsettling mood swings which would often end in minor violence.

---

yow you
'cock' of our yard best fighter in school
wiles cunning persuasive strategies

Men and women

Throughout the 20th century and into the 21st, great changes have been seen in the roles played by men and women in society. At the beginning of the 20th century, women campaigned to win the right to vote in general elections, braving harsh punishments to ensure they were granted equality. In their home lives too, many women have faced struggles to gain recognition for the work that they do.

Male behaviour has also changed as expectations have shifted. From the way they shop to the books they read, men are forging new identities in 21st century society. Increasingly, men and women are working together to create a more equal world.

Extract from a suffragette's account of force-feeding in prison

The suffragettes were women who campaigned in the early 20th century for women to have the right to vote. The direct action they took often led to imprisonment and some suffragettes even went on hunger strike to protest at their treatment. Here, Lady Constance Lytton, a suffragette who was imprisoned in 1910 under the alias of a working-class woman, Jane Wharton, to avoid special treatment, describes how she is force-fed in prison.

I was visited again by the Senior Medical Officer, who asked me how long I had been without food. I said I had eaten a buttered scone and a banana sent in by friends to the police station on Friday at about midnight. He said, "Oh, then, this is the fourth day; that is too long, I shall have to feed you, I must feed you at once," but he went out and nothing happened till about 6 o'clock in the evening, when he returned with, I think, five **wardresses** and the feeding apparatus. He urged me to take food voluntarily. I told him that was absolutely out of the question, that when our **legislators** ceased to resist **enfranchising** women then I should cease to resist taking food in prison. He did not examine my heart nor feel my pulse; he did not ask to do so, nor did I say anything which could possibly induce him to think I would refuse to be examined. I offered no resistance to being placed in position, but lay down voluntarily on the plank bed. Two of the wardresses took hold of my arms, one held my head and one my feet. One wardress helped to pour the food. The doctor leant on my knees as he stooped over my chest to get at my mouth. I shut my mouth and clenched my teeth. I had looked forward to this moment with so much anxiety **lest** my identity should be discovered beforehand, that I felt positively glad when the time had come. The sense of being overpowered by more force than I could possibly resist was complete, but I resisted nothing except with my mouth. The doctor offered me the choice of a wooden or steel gag; he explained elaborately, as he did on most subsequent occasions, that the steel gag would hurt and the wooden one not, and he urged me not to force him to use the steel gag. But I did not speak nor open my mouth, so that after playing about for a moment or two with the wooden one he finally had recourse to the steel. He seemed annoyed at my resistance and he broke into a temper as he plied my teeth with the steel implement. He found that on either side at the back I had false teeth mounted on a bridge which did not take out. The superintending wardress asked if I had any false teeth, if so, that they must be taken out; I made no answer and the process went on. He dug his instrument down on to the sham tooth, it pressed fearfully on the gum. He said if I resisted so much with my teeth, he would have to feed me through the nose. The pain of it was intense and at last I must have given way for he got the gag between my teeth, when he proceeded to turn it much more than necessary until my jaws were fastened wide apart, far more than they could go naturally. Then he put down my throat a tube which seemed to me much too wide and was something like four feet in length. The irritation of the tube was excessive. I choked the moment it touched my throat until it had got down. Then the food was poured in quickly; it made me sick a few seconds after it was down and the action of the sickness made my body and legs double up, but the wardresses instantly pressed back my head and the doctor leant on my knees. The horror of it was more than I can describe. I was sick over the doctor and wardresses, and it seemed a long time before they took the tube out. As the doctor left he gave me a slap on the cheek, not violently, but, as it were, to express his contemptuous disapproval, and he seemed to take for granted that my distress was assumed. At first it seemed such an utterly contemptible thing to have done that I could only laugh in my mind. Then suddenly I saw Jane Warton lying before me, and it seemed as if I were outside of her. She was the most despised, ignorant and helpless prisoner that I had seen. When she had served her time and was out of the prison, no one would believe anything she said, and the doctor when he had fed her by force and tortured her body, struck her on the cheek to show how he despised her! That was Jane Warton, and I had come to help her.

wardresses female prison warders
legislators people making laws
enfranchising giving people the right to vote in elections
lest so that something should not happen

Extract from *Sons and Lovers* by D. H. Lawrence

The following extract is taken from the novel *Sons and Lovers*, which was first published in 1913. Here, Mrs Morel argues with her husband when he returns home from a pub called the Nelson in a drunken state.

Just then Morel came in. He had been very jolly in the Nelson, but coming home had grown irritable. He had not quite got over the feeling of irritability and pain, after having slept on the ground when he was so hot; and a bad conscience afflicted him as he neared the house. He did not know he was angry. But when the garden gate resisted his attempts to open it, he kicked it and broke the latch. He entered just as Mrs. Morel was pouring the infusion of herbs out of the saucepan. Swaying slightly, he lurched against the table. The boiling liquor pitched. Mrs. Morel started back.

"Good gracious," she cried, "coming home in his drunkenness!"

"Comin' home in his what?" he snarled, his hat over his eye.

Suddenly her blood rose in a jet.

"Say you're NOT drunk!" she flashed.

She had put down her saucepan, and was stirring the sugar into the beer. He dropped his two hands heavily on the table, and thrust his face forwards at her.

"'Say you're not drunk,'" he repeated. "Why, nobody but a nasty little bitch like you 'ud 'ave such a thought."

He thrust his face forward at her.

"There's money to **bezzle** with, if there's money for nothing else."

"I've not spent a two-shillin' bit this day," he said.

"You don't get as drunk as a lord on nothing," she replied. "And," she cried, flashing into sudden fury, "if you've been sponging on your beloved Jerry, why, let him look after his children, for they need it."

"It's a lie, it's a lie. Shut your face, woman."

They were now at battle-pitch. Each forgot everything save the hatred of the other and the battle between them. She was fiery and furious as he. They went on till he called her a liar.

"No," she cried, starting up, scarce able to breathe. "Don't call me that — you, the most despicable liar that ever walked in shoe-leather." She forced the last words out of suffocated lungs.

"You're a liar!" he yelled, banging the table with his fist. "You're a liar, you're a liar."

She stiffened herself, with clenched fists.

"The house is filthy with you," she cried.

"Then get out on it — it's mine. Get out on it!" he shouted. "It's me as brings th' money whoam, not thee. It's my house, not **thine**. Then ger out on't — ger out on't!"

"And I would," she cried, suddenly shaken into tears of impotence. "Ah, wouldn't I, wouldn't I have gone long ago, but for those children. Ay, haven't I repented not going years ago, when I'd only the one"— suddenly drying into rage. "Do you think it's for YOU I stop — do you think I'd stop one minute for YOU?"

"Go, then," he shouted, beside himself. "Go!"

"No!" She faced round. "No," she cried loudly, "you shan't have it ALL your own way; you shan't do ALL you like. I've got those children to see to. My word," she laughed, "I should look well to leave them to you."

"Go," he cried thickly, lifting his fist. He was afraid of her. "Go!"

"I should be only too glad. I should laugh, laugh, my lord, if I could get away from you," she replied.

He came up to her, his red face, with its bloodshot eyes, thrust forward, and gripped her arms. She cried in fear of him, struggled to be free. Coming slightly to himself, panting, he pushed her roughly to the outer door, and thrust her forth, slotting the bolt behind her with a bang. Then he went back into the kitchen, dropped into his armchair, his head, bursting full of blood, sinking between his knees. Thus he dipped gradually into a stupor, from exhaustion and intoxication.

---

bezzle a dialect word meaning to eat or drink to excess
thine yours

2

NON-FICTION

Letter to *The Times* newspaper on 'Shop-shyness'

> The following extract is taken from a letter to *The Times* newspaper written by Mr W. Hodgson Burnet and published on the 19th May 1932. Here, Mr Hodson Burnet describes the problem of 'shop-shyness' that he faces whenever he attempts to go shopping.

Sir,

I wonder if any of your male readers suffer as I do from what I can only describe as 'Shop-shyness'? When I go into a shop I never seem to be able to get what I want, and I certainly never want what I eventually get. Take hats. When I want a grey soft hat which I have seen in the window priced at **17s. 6d.** I come out with a *brown* hat (which doesn't suit me) costing **35s**. All because I have not the pluck to insist upon having what I want. I have got into the habit of saying weakly, 'Yes. I'll have that one.' just because the shop assistant assures me that it suits me, fits me, and is a far, far better article than the one I originally asked for.

It is the same with shoes. In a shoe shop I am like clay in the hands of a potter. 'I want a pair of black shoes.' I say,

32

'about twenty-five shillings – like those in the window.' The man kneels down, measures my foot, produces a cardboard box, shoves on a shoe and assures me it is 'a nice fit.' I get up and walk about. 'How much are these?' I ask. 'These are **fifty-two and six**, Sir,' he says, 'a very superior shoe, Sir.' After that I simply *dare* not ask to see the inferior shoes at **25s.**, which is all I had meant to pay. 'Very well,' I say in my weak way, 'I'll take these.' And I do. I also take a bottle of cream polish, a pair of 'gent's **half-hose**,' and some aluminium shoe-trees which the fellow persuades me to let him pack up with the shoes. I have made a mess of my shopping as usual.

Is there any cure for 'shop-shyness'? Is there any 'Course of Shopping Lessons' during which I could as it were 'But while I Learned'? If so I should like to hear of it. For I have just received a price list of 'Very Attractive Gent's Spring Suitings,' and I am afraid – yes I am afraid . . .!

I am, Sir, your obedient servant,
W. HODGSON BURNET

17s. 6d. seventeen shillings and six pence
35s. thirty-five shillings
fifty-two and six fifty-two shillings and six pence
25s. twenty-five shillings
half-hose three-quarter length socks

Extract from a newspaper article in *The Daily Telegraph*

> The following extract is taken from a newspaper article published in *The Daily Telegraph* on the 25th July 2014, exploring changing attitudes towards shopping amongst certain groups of men in the 21st century.

Why are men turning to personal shoppers?

Need help navigating the menswear minefield? Luke Leitch meets the man whose Selfridges' personal shopping service is becoming increasingly popular.

Not long ago, a chap in town from the Middle East spent more than £1 million on clothes (and a watch or two) for himself during a single shopping trip to Selfridges. Or at least that's what I've heard. Asked if that's true, Joe Ottaway will neither confirm nor deny: he merely smiles apologetically from beneath his impressive beard. Discretion, not depilation, is his watchword.

If anyone would know though, it's Ottaway, the stylist in charge of Selfridges's personal shopping service for men. Even though the recommended minimum spend for customers who want Ottaway or one of his three colleagues to guide them through the department store's rails is £2,000, the service has proved extremely popular since launching a few years ago. So popular, in fact, that Selfridges recruited the architect Alex Cochrane to design a just-opened private lounge for high-rolling male shoppers to prepare themselves for the browsing ahead.

According to Ottaway, the role of personal shopper is akin to that of a **sommelier**: "When a guy comes in you have to combine your intuition with your experience and knowledge. We find out everything we can about his tastes, lifestyle, and body-shape. You never know where a man's tastes are going to lead him."

The whole of Selfridge's block-wide first floor is dedicated to masculine clothes and includes the largest men's shoe department in the world. Looking at it all – let along trying it all on – would take at least several days.

My 30-minute pretend-shop with Ottaway, however, provides a near-perfect **precis** of the best new-season menswear – everything from the conventionality of houses like Armani, Tom Ford, Burberry and Zegna through to the radical propositions of edgier designers like Maison Martin Margiela, Sacai and Dries Van Noten.

Rather shamefully – as this is supposed to be my job – I learn about several great new labels I've never heard of before.

Ottaway might be frustratingly discreet – apart from

letting slip about an heir to a throne who wears only Tiger Of Sweden – but he is comfortable spilling the broader beans on the type of men who use him as their shopping sommelier. He says the four main categories are English City types ("aged about 35 to 55"), footballers and loaded visitors from the Middle East and Asia – and their tastes vary dramatically.

Middle Eastern visitors

"One of the key periods for these shoppers, Eid, is coming up. We pull out all the stops for these guys because they might come in only once or twice a year. They are into labels like Givenchy, Louis Vuitton, Balenciaga and Moncler and their tastes are often shaped by what they see R&B and hip-hop stars wearing – it's the Kanye factor!"

Chinese visitors

"Young Chinese guys now make up a huge part of our tax-free shopping, and their tastes are very directional. They are especially keen on accessories: bags and shoes. Their favourite brands tend to be Dior Homme, Prada and Louis Vuitton. Shoe-wise they also love Zanotti as well as Christian Louboutin, Balenciaga and Givenchy."

City types

"These guys practically live in their offices – in fact this afternoon I'm heading to the City to help a client choose some clothes because he doesn't have the time to come in. A lot of them might be quite sheltered, tastewise. They will know about Richard James and Zegna – Zegna practically sells itself – but once we broaden their horizons they might become just as excited about Ralph Lauren Purple Label, Brunello Cucinelli, Brioni and Faconnable."

Footballers

"Footballers are a very self-contained group – they are influenced by each other's tastes. We now do an annual pop-up shop at the training ground of one London premiership club and they love it. They are especially interested in cutting-edge streetwear and extreme embellished trainers like these Zanottis."

---

sommelier a waiter in a restaurant who is in charge of serving wine
precis summary

Extract from *Small Island* by Andrea Levy

The following extract is taken from the novel *Small Island*, which was first published in 2004. The novel is set in London in 1948. Here, Hortense, a Jamaican woman, has travelled to London to join her husband, Gilbert, and has arrived at the house where she believes he is living.

It brought it all back to me. Celia Langley. Celia Langley standing in front of me, her hands on her hips and her head in a cloud. And she is saying: 'Oh, Hortense, when I am older' (all her dreaming began with 'when I am older'). "When I am older, Hortense, I will be leaving Jamaica and I will be going to live in England." This is when her voice became high-class and her nose pointed into the air – well, as far as her round flat nose could – and she swayed as she brought the picture to her mind's eye. "Hortense, in England I will have a big house with a bell at the front door and I will ring the bell." And she make the sound, ding-a-ling, ding-a-ling. "I will ring the bell in this house when I am in England. That is what will happen to me when I am older."

I said nothing at the time. I just nodded and said,

"You surely will, Celia Langley, you surely will!" I did not dare to dream that it would one day be I that would go to England. It would one day be I that would sail on a ship as big as a world and feel the sun's heat on my face gradually change from roasting to caressing. But there was I! Standing at the door of a house in London and ringing the bell. Pushing my finger to hear the ding-a-ling, ding-a-ling. Oh, Celia Langley, where were you then with your big ideas and your nose in the air? Could you see me? Could you see me there in London? Hortense Roberts married with a gold ring and a wedding dress in a trunk. Mrs Joseph. Mrs Gilbert Joseph. What you think of that, Celia Langley? There was I in England ringing the door bell on one of the tallest houses I had ever seen.

But when I pressed this doorbell I did not hear a ring. No ding-a-ling, ding-a-ling. I pressed once more in case the doorbell was not operational. The house, I could see, was shabby. Mark you, shabby in a grand sort of a way. I was sure this house could once have been home to a doctor or a lawyer or perhaps a friend of a friend of the king's. Only the house of someone high-class would have pillars at the doorway. Ornate pillars that twisted with elaborate design. The glass stained with coloured pictures as a church would have. It was true that some were missing, replaced by cardboard and strips of white tape. But who knows what devilish deeds Mr Hitler's bombs carried out during the war? I pushed the doorbell again when it was obvious no one was answering my call. I held my thumb against it and pressed my ear to the window. A light came on now and a woman's voice started calling, "All right, all right, I'm coming! Give us a minute.".

I stepped back down two steps avoiding a small lump of dog's-business that rested in some litter and leaves. I straightened my coat, pulling it closed where I had unfortunately lost a button. I adjusted my hat in case it had sagged in the damp air and left me looking comical. I pulled my back up straight.

The door was answered by an English woman. A blonde-haired, pink cheeked English woman with eyes so blue they were the brightest thing in the street. She looked on my face, parted her slender lips and said, "Yes?"

"Is this the household of Mr Gilbert Joseph?"

"I beg your pardon?"

"Gilbert Joseph?" I said, a little slower.

"Oh, Gilbert. Who are you?" She pronounced Gilbert so strangely that for a moment I was anxious that I would be delivered to the wrong man.

"Mr Gilbert Joseph is my husband - I am his wife."

The woman's face looked puzzled and pleased all at one time. She looked back into the house, lifting her head as she did. Then she turned back to me and said, "Didn't he come to meet you?"

"I have not seen Gilbert," I told her, then went on to ask, "but this is **perchance** where he is **aboding**?

At which this English woman said, "What?" She frowned and looked over my shoulder at the trunk which was resting by the curbside where it had been placed by the driver of the taxi vehicle.

"Is that yours?" she enquired.

"It is."

"It's the size of the Isle of Wight. How did you get it here?" She laughed a little. A gentle giggle that played round her eyes and mouth. I laughed too, so as not to give her the notion that I did not know what she was talking about as regards this 'white island'."

I said, "I came in a taxi cab and the driver assured me that this was the right address. Is this the house of Gilbert Joseph?"

The woman stood for a little while before answering by saying, "Hang on here. I'll see if he's in his room." She then shut the door in my face.

---

perchance by some chance, perhaps
aboding living

41

A speech by Emma Watson

On the 20th September 2014, the actress and UN Women
Goodwill Ambassador, Emma Watson, made a speech at
the United Nations Headquarters in New York to launch
her 'HeForShe' campaign for gender equality.

Today we are launching a campaign called 'HeForShe'.

I am reaching out to you because I need your help. We
want to end gender inequality—and to do that we need
everyone to be involved.

This is the first campaign of its kind at the UN: we want
to try and galvanize as many men and boys as possible to
be advocates for gender equality. And we don't just want
to talk about it, but make sure it is tangible.

I was appointed six months ago and the more I
have spoken about feminism the more I have realized
that fighting for women's rights has too often become
synonymous with man-hating. If there is one thing I
know for certain, it is that this has to stop.

For the record, feminism by definition is: "The belief
that men and women should have equal rights and
opportunities. It is the theory of the political, economic
and social equality of the sexes."

I started questioning gender-based assumptions when

at eight I was confused at being called "bossy," because I wanted to direct the plays we would put on for our parents—but the boys were not.

When at 14 I started being sexualized by certain elements of the press.

When at 15 my girlfriends started dropping out of their sports teams because they didn't want to appear "muscly."

When at 18 my male friends were unable to express their feelings.

I decided I was a feminist and this seemed uncomplicated to me. But my recent research has shown me that feminism has become an unpopular word.

Apparently I am among the ranks of women whose expressions are seen as too strong, too aggressive, isolating, anti-men and, unattractive.

Why is the word such an uncomfortable one?

I am from Britain and think it is right that as a woman I am paid the same as my male counterparts. I think it is right that I should be able to make decisions about my own body. I think it is right that women be involved on my behalf in the policies and decision-making of my country. I think it is right that socially I am afforded the same respect as men. But sadly I can say that there is no one country in the world where all women can expect to receive these rights.

No country in the world can yet say they have achieved gender equality.

These rights I consider to be human rights but I am one of the lucky ones. My life is a sheer privilege because my parents didn't love me less because I was born a daughter. My school did not limit me because I was a girl. My mentors didn't assume I would go less far because I might give birth to a child one day. These influencers were the gender equality ambassadors that made me who I am today. They may not know it, but they are the inadvertent feminists who are changing the world today. And we need more of those.

And if you still hate the word—it is not the word that is important but the idea and the ambition behind it. Because not all women have been afforded the same rights that I have. In fact, statistically, very few have been.

In 1995, Hilary Clinton made a famous speech in Beijing about women's rights. Sadly many of the things she wanted to change are still a reality today.

But what stood out for me the most was that only 30 per cent of her audience were male. How can we affect change in the world when only half of it is invited or feel welcome to participate in the conversation?

Men—I would like to take this opportunity to extend your formal invitation. Gender equality is your issue too.

Because to date, I've seen my father's role as a parent being valued less by society despite my needing his presence as a child as much as my mother's.

I've seen young men suffering from mental illness

unable to ask for help for fear it would make them look less "macho"—in fact in the UK suicide is the biggest killer of men between 20-49 years of age; eclipsing road accidents, cancer and coronary heart disease. I've seen men made fragile and insecure by a distorted sense of what constitutes male success. Men don't have the benefits of equality either.

We don't often talk about men being imprisoned by gender stereotypes but I can see that they are and that when they are free, things will change for women as a natural consequence.

If men don't have to be aggressive in order to be accepted women won't feel compelled to be submissive. If men don't have to control, women won't have to be controlled.

Both men and women should feel free to be sensitive. Both men and women should feel free to be strong . . . It is time that we all perceive gender on a spectrum not as two opposing sets of ideals.

If we stop defining each other by what we are not and start defining ourselves by what we are—we can all be freer and this is what HeForShe is about. It's about freedom.

I want men to take up this mantle. So their daughters, sisters and mothers can be free from prejudice but also so that their sons have permission to be vulnerable and human too—reclaim those parts of themselves they abandoned and in doing so be a more true and complete version of themselves.

You might be thinking who is this Harry Potter girl? And what is she doing up on stage at the UN. It's a good question and trust me, I have been asking myself the same thing. I don't know if I am qualified to be here. All I know is that I care about this problem. And I want to make it better.

And having seen what I've seen—and given the chance—I feel it is my duty to say something. English Statesman Edmund Burke said: "All that is needed for the forces of evil to triumph is for enough good men and women to do nothing."

In my nervousness for this speech and in my moments of doubt I've told myself firmly—if not me, who, if not now, when. If you have similar doubts when opportunities are presented to you I hope those words might be helpful.

Because the reality is that if we do nothing it will take 75 years, or for me to be nearly a hundred before women can expect to be paid the same as men for the same work. 15.5 million girls will be married in the next 16 years as children. And at current rates it won't be until 2086 before all rural African girls will be able to receive a secondary education.

If you believe in equality, you might be one of those inadvertent feminists I spoke of earlier.

And for this I applaud you.

We are struggling for a uniting word but the good news is we have a uniting movement. It is called HeForShe. I am inviting you to step forward, to be seen to speak up, to be the "he" for "she". And to ask yourself if not me, who? If not now, when?

Thank you.

Newspaper editorial about gender-specific books

The following editorial was published in the *Independent on Sunday* newspaper in March 2014 to explain its decision to no longer review books aimed specifically at boys or girls.

Gender-specific books demean all our children.

A good read is just that. Ask any child, regardless of gender, says *Independent on Sunday* literary editor Katy Guest.

Sugar and spice and all things nice, that's what little girls are made of. And boys? They're made of trucks and trains and aeroplanes, building blocks, chemistry experiments, sword fights and guns, football, cricket, running and jumping, adventure and ideas, games, farts and snot, and pretty much anything else they can think of.

At least, that's the impression that children are increasingly given by the very books that are supposed to broaden their horizons.

An online campaign called Let Books Be Books, which

petitions publishers to ditch gender-specific children's books, has met with mixed success recently. Last week, both Parragon (which sells Disney titles, among others) and Usborne (the Independent Publisher of the Year 2014), agreed that they will no longer publish books specifically titled "for boys" or "for girls". Unfortunately, Michael O'Mara, which owns Buster Books, pledged to continue segregating young readers according to their gender. Mr O'Mara himself told *The Independent* that their *Boys' Book* covers "things like how to make a bow and arrow and how to play certain sports and you'd get things about style and how to look cool in the girls' book." At the same time, he added: "We would never publish a book that demeaned one sex or the other".

It is not like a publisher to leave a bandwagon unjumped upon, but Mr O'Mara seems to have missed a trick. Hasn't he heard of Suzanne Collins' multi-million-selling *Hunger Games* trilogy, which has a female lead character and striking, non-pink cover designs, and is loved by boys and girls equally? For anyone else who has missed it, the heroine, Katniss Everdeen, is rather handy with a bow and arrow and doesn't spend much time caring about looking cool. At the same time, Mr O'Mara should know that telling boys they should all be interested in doing physical activities outdoors, while girls should be interested in how they look, is demeaning to both.

There are those who will say that insisting on gender-neutral books and toys for children is a bizarre experiment in social engineering by radical lefties and paranoid "femininazis" who won't allow boys to be boys, and girls to be girls. (Because, by the way, seeking equality of rights and opportunities was a key plank of Nazi ideology, was it?) But the "experiment" is nothing new. When I grew up in the 1970s, and when my parents grew up in the 1950s, brothers and sisters shared the same toys, books and games, which came in many more colours than just pink and blue, and there was no obvious disintegration of society as a result. Publishers and toy companies like to say that they are offering parents more "choice" these days by billing some of their products as just for boys and others as just for girls. What they're actually doing, by convincing children that boys and girls can't play with each other's stuff, is forcing parents to buy twice as much stuff.

There are also those who argue that children are set upon their boyish and girly courses from conception, and that no amount of book-reading is going to change them. In fact, there is no credible evidence that boys and girls are born with innately different enthusiasms, and plenty of evidence that their tastes are acquired through socialisation. Let's face it, any company with a billion dollar advertising budget could convince even Jeremy Clarkson to dress up as a Disney princess if it really wanted to, and probably would if his doing so could double its income. So what hope is there against all this pressure for an impressionable child?

I wouldn't mind, but splitting children's books strictly along gender lines is not even good publishing. Just like other successful children's books, *The Hunger Games* was not aimed at girls or boys; like JK Rowling, Roald Dahl, Robert Muchamore and others, Collins just wrote great stories, and readers bought them in their millions. Now, Dahl's *Matilda* is published with a pink cover, and I have heard one bookseller report seeing a mother snatching a copy from her small son's hands saying "That's for girls" as she replaced it on the shelf.

You see, it is not just girls' ambitions that are being frustrated by the limiting effects of "books for girls", in which girls' roles are all passive, domestic and in front of a mirror. Rebecca Davies, who writes the children's books blog at Independent.co.uk, tells me that she is equally sick of receiving "books which have been commissioned solely for the purpose of 'getting boys reading' [and which have] all-male characters and thin, action-based plots." What we are doing by pigeon-holing children is badly letting them down. And books, above all things, should be available to any child who is interested in them.

Happily, as the literary editor of *The Independent on Sunday*, there is something that I can do about this. So I promise now that the newspaper and this website will not be reviewing any book which is explicitly aimed at just girls, or just boys. Nor will *The Independent*'s books section. And nor will the children's books blog at Independent.co.uk. Any Girls' Book of Boring Princesses that crosses my desk will go straight into the recycling pile along with every Great Big Book of Snot for Boys. If you are a publisher with enough faith in your new book that you think it will appeal to all children, we'll be very happy to hear from you. But the next Harry Potter or Katniss Everdeen will not come in glittery pink covers. So we'd thank you not to send us such books at all.

The World of Work

As the pace of change has accelerated in the 20th and 21st centuries, the world of work has been transformed, with new fields of employment created and other jobs changed beyond recognition. Some professions, such as wheelwrights and blacksmiths, haven't survived these changes in society, whilst others, such as the working life of the shepherd, have remained relatively unchanged.

New technologies have created new types of career and also changed the ways in which people work, with email and Skype enabling people to work from home or hold 'virtual' meetings. The 20th century also saw a huge increase in the number of careers open to women in the workplace, with women finding employment in roles that had been traditionally viewed as male professions.

An account by Jubal Merton, wheelwright and blacksmith

The following extract is taken from *Akenfield: Portrait of an English Village* by Ronald Blythe, which was first published in 1969. In this book, Blythe collected together accounts from the residents of his local village, charting working life in the first half of the 20th century and describing many jobs which have since disappeared. Here, Jubal Merchant, aged sixty, describes how he learned to become a wheelwright and blacksmith.

I've lived in the village all my life. I've never been away. I left school in 1922, when I was thirteen, and was apprenticed to my father and my uncle, who owed these premises. My father was the wheelwright and my uncle was the blacksmith. I was the only apprentice and they were very strict. 'You've got to have a good eye,' they said. 'Everything that's got to be done in **wheelwrighting** has got to be done by the eye. You've got to let your eye be your guide.' They were right, of course. When you get the hub of a wheel it has to be **morticed** once and only once first go.

The first job I had to do was to make spokes, and sometimes I was allowed to saw out the shafts for the

tumbrils. All the shafts were cut out by handsaw from heavy planks of wood about ¾ inches thick and about two feet wide. We planed these and shaped them up fine. Heaps of times I did a shaft and I'd think, 'That's lovely!' Then my father would rub his hand up it and say, 'Why, boy, it ain't *half* done!' He was a first-class wheelwright and was known all over Suffolk and my grandfather and great-grandfather were the same. They all worked in this same shop and the wagons they made lie about in the farmyards. They ain't used but they can't wear out. When I got so I could use a plane and a wheel-shave, I started to make wheelbarrows. They were a difficult job, a most difficult job indeed. Especially the front pieces which we called the stumps. The stump was another thing you had to cut right first time else it was no good. There was no second chance in so much of what we did. It made us cautious but at the same time it made us willing to take a risk. It was as much in the eye as in the hand. There was a moment when you had to say *now*! Then you could breathe again […]

When I had helped to make a wagon I had to learn to paint it. We did everything in this shop, you see. The farmers were most particular about the painting. The colours were all bought in Ipswich. There was red lead and vegetable black, white lead, which was like thick distemper, and there was Chinese red and Venetian red, all these were the old colours used by the wagon-makers.

The bodywork was all painted blue. Always blue. The blue rode well in the corn. The wheels were done in Chinese red and lined-out with Venetian red, which was marvellously expensive – about £1 an ounce. We mixed all the paints here. Paint for small jobs was ground on a little stone, but if we had a lot to do we ground it in a paint-mill. Nothing whatever was wasted of anything. You had to grind paint very, very slowly so that the mill didn't warm up. If it did it would discolour the paint. The farmers were very proud of their wagons and tumbrils and would wash them down every week-end. Some of them had to go to Ipswich two or three times a week and they had to look fine. A tumbril could travel with about two tons a time. They were beautiful and they had to be kept beautiful. They weren't very expensive. My father made tumbrils for £12 a time when he was a young man. When I first started making them they cost £25 – that is a one-horse tumbril. A wagon would cost about £40. Once they were finished they lasted for ever. The village was full of wagons a hundred years old or more when I was a boy, and still perfect.

---

wheelwrighting building or repairing wooden wheels
mortice to make a deep notch or recess in a piece of wood
tumbril farmer's cart

Extract from *The Shepherd's Life* by James Rebanks

In the following extract from his memoir *The Shepherd's Life*, which was first published in 2015, James Rebanks describes his life as a shepherd, an occupation essentially unchanged for centuries.

I love lambing time. In the long, sodden and wind-lashed winter weeks, I sometimes daydream of escaping the muddy tedium, but I wouldn't want to miss lambing. I've always loved it, ever since I used to follow my grandad around, helping him feed the ewes in pens of little hay bales, sometimes being given one to lamb like my daughters do now.

I always marvel at how gentle some of the men were at this time of year, how you saw them kneeling in the mud or the straw of the pens, delicately threading a stomach tube down an ailing lamb's throat, over the little pink tongue. You could see how much they cared. My dad would be gutted if he lost a lamb; it would hang over him like a grey cloud until he had put things right by saving others.

We start lambing at the beginning of April. In theory,

this is the point at which winter becomes spring here, but sometimes winter isn't aware of our plans and the weather is still gruesome. Snow. Rain. Hail. Wind. Mud. One morning, by the time I get to the first field of lambing ewes, I am already wet. The rain is biting cold and the hillsides are just sheets of water. It is a disaster zone. A first-time ewe (a shearling) has dropped her lamb, when giving birth, into the **beck**, where it is stumbling and falling back into the shallow but deadly water. It is tough, but looks close to giving up, as it cannot climb up the bank.

I lift it out and put it in the trailer. I send Floss to hold the ewe up, and after some slipping and sliding in the mud I have hold of her. I will take them home to shelter. The ewe looks uncertain of her lamb now, like the thread between them has broken. A hundred yards away, on either side of me, lie new lambs that look as if they are dead or dying. There is nowhere for even the experienced ewes to hide their newborn lambs from this downpour. Normally dry places behind walls have turned into streams, sheltered spots are now ponds. The temperature is murderous. My neighbour says later this is the worst lambing weather she has ever experienced.

The first lamb I touch feels stiff and cold, just a faint hint of warmth on its bluing tongue. I lower it despondently into the trailer. The next two, from an older ewe that has tried to get them up and licked dry, have some life in them but are fading fast, their core temperature dropping. Desperate measures are needed. I decide to save the lambs quickly and worry about the ewes later. After two minutes, I have gathered up five lambs and am on the road home.

Another ewe has lambed under a wall and had two proper strong lambs with big bold heads and white ear tips visible even in the mud. With a full trailer, I have to leave them to their mother's attention, but she is an old, experienced ewe and knows the game. I meet a friend coming the other way from his own flock. We exchange blasphemies.

Minutes later, I have the lambs tight under a heat lamp, hung so low it is burning off the slime, mud and afterbirth. I haven't much hope for any of them. The first one is stiffening like a corpse. There doesn't seem to be much to lose, so I stomach-tube it with some warm artificial **colostrum**, figuring something warm inside may help. But sometimes the shock of the milk is too much for them – I am gambling. I leave my wife, Helen, drying them with towels from the bathroom. The children get themselves ready for school. Chaos. I go back for the mothers.

The fields are so sodden I am on my backside more often than I am on my feet. Only the bravery of Floss lets me catch them: with no lamb to hold their attention they are free to gallop off. I fill the trailer with the required ewes (making a mental note which lambs they have each given birth to). Telling which ewes have lambed is made easier because they have a bit of blood or afterbirth on their tail, and they will usually hold to the place where they gave birth.

I go back to the barn where Helen has managed to get some life into the lambs, and an hour later, miraculously, they are all sitting up and warm. Each is penned with its mother, bedded with clean straw. The one that was in the beck is suckling its mother. By the time we have tended to them and had a bit of breakfast, shoved the kids on the school bus, wearing the wrong clothes, it is time to get back to the first lambing field to do the rounds again.

---

beck stream
colostrum a form of milk produced by mammals
immediately after giving birth

The Road to Nab End by William Woodruff

In the following extract from his autobiography *The Road to Nab End*, William Woodruff describes his early working experiences as a newspaper delivery boy in Lancashire in the 1920s.

While we were living at Livingstone Road I really began to earn my keep. I took pride in doing so. I started delivering morning and evening newspapers for George and Madge Latham, a young, childless couple in their thirties, who ran a sweets, tobacco and newspaper business on Revidge Road. The Lathams were an honest, hard-working couple. They were Lancashire folk: active, tough, resourceful. They were always cheerful. I was a year below the minimum age, but they took me on just the same; no one enforced the law. They paid me the princely sum of two shillings and sixpence per week, of which I kept a dodger. Mother took the rest. That was my contribution to help pay for the house.

I came to spend so much time with the Lathams that home and school fell into the background. Winter and summer, wet or fine, I got myself up at five to meet George at the newspaper depot in the centre of town about a mile and a half away. I had to run through the dark, hushed streets for half an hour or so. I'd find him waiting for me with his bicycle. On cold mornings his teeth were chattering. Together, we then fought our way in and out of an ill-lit warehouse that served as the newspaper depot. It was a daily hand-to-hand battle with other men to get our newspapers. It was bedlam there.

Once we'd got the warm, damp bundles under our arms, we loaded them and George's bike onto the first tram to Revidge Road at six o'clock. Kneeling on the ribbed floor, we sorted the papers as the tram lurched along. When the floor was wet with melted snow off people's clogs, we used the seats. At Revidge Road, George helped me off the tram. With a bag of newspapers on either shoulder, I began my round. Depending on the weather, I'd be running through the streets for the next hour, or hour and a half. I found it wonderful to have the world to myself.

I had no difficulty knowing which paper went where. Labour people took the *Herald* or *News Chronicle*, conservatives the *Mail* or the *Telegraph*, liberals the *Guardian*, the toffs took *The Times*. A switch in newspaper usually meant a switch in political allegiance. I knew how my customers would vote.

Delivering newspapers taught me a lot about human nature. I learned to recognize the news addicts and the insomniacs. In summer, these chaps paced up and down their lawns awaiting my arrival. The way they snatched the paper out of my hand, made me feel important. I knew by the way they rushed to the financial pages that, like most of the rich, they were fearful of losing their money. I'd nothing to lose so the financial crashes left me unmoved. I decided it must be worrying to be rich.

In bad weather, the kind-hearted awaited my arrival with a cup of tea and a bun. The not so kind angrily waved the paper in my face as if I were responsible for the success of Labour at the polls, or the assassination of the head of a foreign state. I felt like saying: 'Look, Mister, I don't write these papers, I just deliver them.' Usually, I kept my mouth shut. One thing I did learn was never to give a man the wrong paper. You've no idea how touchy some people can be. They'd bawl me out as if I'd permanently committed them to the wrong religion.

In time I came to have a large family of newspaper readers. I knew them more closely than they realized. I knew them by the way their houses stared, sat and slept. I closely followed my customers' births, weddings, divorces and deaths. I knew who had gone broke, and who was doing very nicely. I knew when a move was under way. I delivered Dr Michael's paper. He was the great ear, nose and throat specialist who was unable to save his own daughter from a fatal ear infection. 'And how is the Michael child?' some customers asked me as if I were a consulting physician.

With a passion for the printed word, I not only delivered newspapers, I read them too. I started every day eager to see what the world was up to. One morning in 1927 I was thrilled to read about Lindbergh's solo flight from the United States to France. My friends and I didn't stop talking about Lucky Lindy. The only aeroplanes we had seen were three single-engine aircraft flown by a group of American rough riders who came for three days to barnstorm from a field on the edge of town. They charged five shillings for a ten minute ordeal. My mates and I saw the whole show and were awestruck. The planes were thumped and banged about so much that we expected them to fall apart. When we saw people getting out and throwing up, we concluded that it was just as well that nobody was pressing a free ride on us.

The newspapers were full of politics. That's how I first heard about Mussolini in Italy and Stalin in Russia. I cut their pictures out of the paper and lined them up like a rogues' gallery on my bedroom wall. With the world depression in trade and industry at its height, the papers also had a lot to say about commercial crises, strikes and lockouts.

Sometimes the news was so arresting that I stopped under a street light to read it. Banner headlines greeted the formation of a second Labour government in 1929. We believed that Labour would put things right this time. Ramsay MacDonald was to be Prime Minister.

One thing I did learn, was the way newspapers contradicted each other – that truth is not as straightforward as I thought it was. A disaster in politics in one paper was a victory in another. I asked myself how could that be? I also learned to be suspicious of the writers who had a simple answer for everything. Every day I read the column by Hannan Swaffer in the *Daily Herald*. Why, if they'd have put Mr Swaffer in charge, the country and the world would have been on its feet again in seven days. I found it confusing.

I asked George Latham what he made of it; after all, he had newsprint all over his hands as I did, and he was much older.

'I'd never deliver the news, Billy, if I tried to make head or tail of it,' he answered. 'We're businessmen, Billy. We have our work cut out delivering papers without worrying about what it all means.'

Extract from *The Edible Woman* by Margaret Atwood

The following extract is taken from the novel *The Edible Woman*, which was first published in 1969. Here, the narrator, a young woman named Marian McAlpin, describes her work in a market research firm.

The humidity was worse inside. I waded among the ladies' desks to my own corner and had scarcely settled in behind the typewriter before the backs of my legs were stuck to the black leatherette of the chair. The air-conditioning system, I saw, had failed again, though since it is merely a fan which revolves in the centre of the ceiling, stirring the air around like spoon in soup, it makes little difference whether it is going or not. But it was evidently bad for the ladies' morale to see the blades dangling up there unmoving: it created the impression that nothing was being done, spurring their **inertia** on to even greater **stasis**. They squatted at their desks, toad-like and sluggish, blinking and opening and closing their mouths. Friday is always a bad day at the office.

I had begun to peck **languidly** at my damp typewriter when Mrs. Withers, the dietician, marched in through the back door, drew up, and scanned the room. She wore her usual Betty Grable hairdo and open-toed pumps, and her shoulders had an aura of shoulder pads even in a sleeveless dress. 'Ah, Marian,' she said, 'you're just in time. I need another pre-test taster for the canned rice pudding study, and none of the ladies seem very hungry this morning.'

She wheeled and headed briskly for the kitchen. There is something unwiltable about dieticians. I unstuck myself from the chair, feeling like a volunteer singled out from the ranks; but I reminded myself that my stomach could use the extra breakfast.

In the tiny immaculate kitchen she explained her problem while spooning equal portions of canned rice pudding into three glass bowls. 'You work on questionnaires, Marian, maybe you can help us. We can't decide whether to have them taste all three flavours at the same meal, or each flavour separately at subsequent meals. Or perhaps we could have them taste in pairs – say, Vanilla and Orange at one meal, and Vanilla and Caramel at another. Of course we want to get as unbiased a sampling as possible, and so much depends on what else has been served – the colours of the vegetables for instance, and the tablecloth.'

I sampled the Vanilla.

'How would you rate the colour on that?' she asked anxiously, pencil poised. 'Natural, Somewhat Artificial, or Definitely Unnatural?'

67

'Have you thought about putting raisins in it?' I said, turning to the Caramel. I didn't wish to offend her.

'Raisins are too risky,' she said. 'Many don't like them.'

I set down the Caramel and tried the Orange. 'Are you going to have them serve it hot?' I asked. 'Or maybe with cream?'

'Well, it's intended primarily for the time-saver market,' she said. 'They naturally would want to serve it cold. They can add cream if they like, later, I mean we've nothing really against it though it's not nutritionally necessary, it's fortified with vitamins already, but right now we want a *pure* taste-test.'

'I think subsequent meals would be best,' I said.

'If we could only do it in the middle of the afternoon. But we need a family reaction . . .' She tapped her pencil thoughtfully on the edge of the stainless steel sink.

'Yes, well,' I said. 'I'd better be getting back.' Deciding for them what they wanted to know wasn't part of my job.

Sometimes I wonder just which things are part of my job, especially when I find myself calling up garage mechanics to ask them about their pistons and gaskets or handing out pretzels to suspicious old ladies on street corners. I know what Seymour Surveys hired me as – I'm supposed to spend my time revising the questionnaires, turning the **convoluted** and overly-subtle prose of the psychologists who write them into simple questions which can be understood by the people who ask them as well as the people who answer them. A question like 'In what **percentile** would you place the visual impact value?' is not useful. When I got the job after graduation I considered myself lucky – it was better than many but after four months its limits are still vaguely defined.

inertia being inert or slow to take action
stasis state of inactivity
languidly slowly, without energy
convoluted overly complicated
percentile a measure used in statistics

Extract from a newspaper article in *The Guardian*

The following extract is taken from a newspaper article in *The Guardian*, published on the 26th October 2011, and looks at the skills needed to become a software engineer.

Becoming a software engineer: from Silicon Valley to Shoreditch

Software engineer Tony Chen's career has taken him from Silicon Valley to Silicon Roundabout in Shoreditch. He describes the skills, expertise and approach that have helped him get ahead.

It's Tuesday afternoon, and my boss just gave us the news that we're doing another site re-design and we have one month to do it. Our team moans because we know it's going to be a lot of hard work – maybe 50 or 60 hour weeks for the next four weeks, but we know it's critical to the company's success. In the life of a software start-up, speed is king. How quickly a business can adapt and change their hypothesis on what a consumer's wants and needs are, and then execute that vision impacts on the company's chance of success. What most people don't know is many companies start out with a preliminary vision, and only through time and various trials and tribulations, do they finally get to a sustainable and successful business model.

Flickr started as an online gaming company, YouTube was a dating site, and Nintendo originally started out as a trading card company. What's interesting about the software industry, especially the ones that are built on the internet, is that it takes virtually no capital to get started, it's easy to switch gears and **iterate** on the product.

As a software engineer, you are usually well-versed in either backend or front end engineering – sometimes even both. A backend engineer's primary job is to write code that will quickly analyse, filter and retrieve an enormous amount of data and give a result back to the user within seconds or a sub-second (think Google search, loading your Facebook feed, or finding directions between two places). A front end engineer's job is to make the site beautiful and handle all the interactions between the users and the interface (like Farmville game play, Google maps, and web page animations and transitions in general).

I found my first full time job through a career fair at college in San Diego. The company flew me up to the Silicon Valley for an all day interview. The typical engineering interview questions pertain more to your ability to problem solve, and have less emphasis on your personality. Unless you are really confident, some studying is recommended. Remember that coding questions usually should have quick and short answers. If you are taking longer than 5 minutes to get to a solution, you might be over thinking it. If you ever do get stuck during an interview, try and vocalise what you are thinking to the interviewer. Sometimes that alone will be enough for the interviewer to drop you some helpful hints as they listen to your thought process.

Six years into my career, I just relocated to London to join Songkick, a music startup based at Silicon Roundabout in Shoreditch. For me, it's obvious that the music industry needs change, and one of the great things about being at a startup is to help drive that change through the consumer. Songkick helps users track their favourite musicians so that they never miss a concert by sending personalised concert alerts whenever favourite artists are coming to town. The day to day working environment is great. The dress code is informal, there is a Tesco delivery in the mornings so the fridge is always stocked, and each employee receives a monthly gig allowance.

I have had the privilege of working at four very different startups all within various company life cycles. While each had its innovations, they had their fair share of challenges as well. As an engineer, you're often given tasks to build features that a consumer will directly interact with, such as: a new game element, a preview mode for the book that you've been putting together online, or a shiny new graph that helps you track your financial progress. But at a startup, you may have the urge to dig deeper and go beyond your assigned tasks. There's often an open forum for discussion between engineers, product managers, and designers as you work together to get the best product out. This could mean sacrificing nice to have features in favour of delivering a focused and easy to use user experience. In addition, you'll always be finding new ways to optimise every step along the way. In terms of speed, every 0.2 seconds count. Why 200 milliseconds? It takes the brain roughly 200 milliseconds to recognise facial expressions, and is equivalent to what a user considers an action to be instant.

Growing up in the Silicon Valley, I was either destined to become an engineer or at the very least work for an engineering company. Everyone is always looking for the latest and greatest iPhone app, following to see what Google, Facebook, and Twitter are doing next, or keeping up with emerging startups. Even non-engineers follow these trends because it's part of our culture. The technology industry is ever-changing and knowledge is the key to survival.

---

iterate create a new version

Extract from *Microserfs* by Douglas Coupland

> The following extract is taken from the opening of the
> novel *Microserfs*, which was first published in 1995. Set in
> the headquarters of Microsoft in Washington in the United
> States and presented as a series of diary entries, the novel
> is narrated by Daniel and describes his working life.

FRIDAY Early Fall, 1993

This morning, just after 11:00, Michael locked himself
into his office and he won't come out.

Bill (Bill!) sent Michael this totally wicked **flame-mail**
from hell on the e-mail system – and he just **wailed on**
a chunk of code Michael had written. Using the *Bloom
County*-cartoons-taped-on-the-door index, Michael is
certainly the most sensitive coder in Building Seven – not
the type to take criticism easily. Exactly why Bill would
choose Michael of all people to wail on is confusing.

We figured it must have been a random quality check
to keep the troops in line. Bill's so smart.

Bill is wise.

Bill is kind.

Bill is benevolent.

Bill, Be My Friend . . . *Please!*

Actually, nobody on our floor has ever been flamed by Bill personally. The episode was tinged with glamour and we were somewhat jealous. I tried to tell Michael this, but he was crushed.

Shortly before lunch he stood like a lump outside my office. His skin was pale like rising bread dough, and his Toppy's cut was dripping sweat, leaving little damp marks on the oyster-gray-with-plum highlights of the Microsoft carpeting. He handed me a printout of Bill's memo and then **gallumphed** into his office, where he's been burrowed ever since.

He won't answer his phone, respond to e-mail, or open his door. On his doorknob he placed a "Do Not Disturb" thingy stolen from the **Boston Radisson** during last year's Macworld **Expo**. Todd and I walked out onto the side lawn to try to peek in his window, but his Venetian blinds were closed and a gardener with a leaf blower chased us away with a spray of grass clippings.

They mow the lawn every ten minutes at Microsoft. It looks like green Lego pads.

Finally, at about 2:30AM, Todd and I got concerned about Michael's not eating, so we drove to the 24-hour Safeway in Redmond. We went shopping for "flat" foods to slip underneath Michael's door.

The Safeway was completely empty save for us and a few other Microsoft people just like us – hair-trigger geeks in pursuit of just the right snack. Because of all the rich nerds living around here, Redmond and Bellevue are very "on-demand" neighbourhoods. Nerds get what they want when they want it, and they go psycho if it's not immediately available. Nerds overfocus. I guess that's the problem. But it's precisely this ability to narrow-focus that makes them so good at code writing: one line at a time, one line in a strand of millions.

flame-mail a nasty email criticizing somebody
wail on attack, batter
gallumph move clumsily
Boston Radisson a hotel in Boston
Expo a trade fair where companies showcase their products

Rich and poor

In the 20th century and into the 21st, a huge gap exists between the lives of the rich and the poor. From the problems faced by the people living in poverty to the concerns of the wealthy, their respective worlds would appear completely alien to each other.

In many ways, in the hundred and so years that span the period covered by this book, the lives of the homeless have not changed. From the dangers faced when sleeping rough on the streets to the health problems that both cause and result from homelessness, the accounts in this book reveal the harsh conditions of the homeless life.

For the very wealthy, such concerns may seem very remote. However, the extracts included in this collection reveal not only the lifestyles of the rich, but also the problems that they face.

Extract from *Down and Out in Paris and London* by George Orwell

> The following extract is taken from *Down and Out in Paris and London*, a memoir by the writer George Orwell of his experiences of homelessness and poverty, which was first published in 1933.

On the way to Edbury I told Paddy that I had a friend from whom I could be sure of getting money, and suggested going straight into London rather than face another night in the **spike**. But Paddy had not been in Edbury spike recently, and, tramp-like, he would not waste a night's free lodging. We arranged to go into London the next morning. I had only a halfpenny, but Paddy had two shillings, which would get us a bed each and a few cups of tea.

The Edbury spike did not differ much from the one at Romton. The worst feature was that all tobacco was confiscated at the gate, and we were warned that any man caught smoking would be turned out at once. Under the Vagrancy Act tramps can be prosecuted for smoking in the spike – in fact, they can be prosecuted for almost anything; but the authorities generally save the trouble of a prosecution by turning disobedient men out of doors. There was no work to do, and the cells were fairly comfortable. We slept two in a cell, 'one up, one down' – that is, one on a wooden shelf and one on the floor, with straw palliasses and plenty of blankets, dirty but not **verminous**. The food was the same as at Romton, except that we had tea instead of cocoa. One could get extra tea in the morning, as the Tramp Major was selling it at a halfpenny a mug, illicitly no doubt. We were each given a hunk of bread and cheese to take away for our midday meal.

When we got into London we had eight hours to kill before the lodging-houses opened. It is curious how one does not notice things. I had been in London innumerable times, and yet till that day I had never noticed one of the worst things about London – the fact that it costs money even to sit down. In Paris, if you had no money and could not find a public bench, you would sit on the pavement. Heaven knows what sitting on the pavement would lead to in London – prison, probably. By four we had stood five hours, and our feet seemed red-hot from the hardness of the stones. We were hungry, having eaten our ration as soon as we left the spike, and I was out of tobacco – it mattered less to Paddy, who picked up cigarette ends. We tried two churches and found them locked. Then we tried a public library, but there were no seats in it. As a last hope Paddy suggested trying a **Rowton House**; by the rules they would not let us in before seven, but we might slip in unnoticed. We walked up to the magnificent doorway (the Rowton Houses really are magnificent) and very casually, trying to look like regular lodgers, began to stroll in. Instantly a man lounging in the doorway, a sharp-faced fellow, evidently in some position of authority, barred the way.

'You men sleep 'ere last night?'

'No.'

'Then – off.'

We obeyed, and stood two more hours on the street corner. It was unpleasant, but it taught me not to use the expression 'street corner loafer', so I gained something from it.

---

spike a shelter of last resort used by the homeless
verminous infested with vermin
Rowton House a chain of hostels in London

Extract from *Shivering Denizens of His Mad Realm,* an essay by Will Nicoll

> The following extract is taken from an essay by the British writer and journalist Will Nicoll. Here, the writer describes spending a night on the streets of Edinburgh and hearing the stories of the homeless there.

Bristo Square is a vast Gothic courtyard outside Edinburgh University, adorned with dark granite gargoyles. It's night-time, and the thoroughfare between the buildings is busy. Three young women in stilettos and white suede cowboy hats, trimmed with pink fur, stumble past; unnoticed, street people criss-cross the revellers. Some are young refugees, care leavers or migrant workers; many are gnarled old rough sleepers, who carry their belongings in plastic bags. A few scream abuse at passing students, but most walk on, fearful and quiet, with their eyes fixed on the buildings ahead. All belong to a silent underclass who exist quietly and painfully in every city.

There are an estimated 1,700 rough sleepers in Scotland. Edinburgh, with more than 360, is their capital.

As the sun falls behind the mosque's turquoise dome, the street people make their way towards Magdalene House – a soup kitchen known by only the destitute. As I push open the heavy wooden door, with its weary hinges and reinforced glass panels, I smell tonic wine, lentil soup, and turpentine. It's being redecorated, and the pine panels on the walls have peeled, revealing craters of pastel-pink paint.

Inside, there are men with thick, dark beards and beetroot-red faces, and men who are jaundiced and yellow, with wide, bloodshot eyes and lank, thinning hair. There are atrophied soldiers – drunk on white spirit – and old sea captains, who wear their war wounds like ghost stories. Some scowl, or shudder, as they pick tobacco flakes from their gold-capped teeth; others flinch like mice caught near the tracks of a runaway freight train, as the night air fills the room.

"We used to get them, back when they were on the methylated spirits," a woman says, as she dispenses soup from behind the serving counter. She glances at me and smiles as she butters bread. "Now it's white cider. It's the same thing if you ask me."

I sit at a table beside John – a musician who has just returned to Scotland from America. He tells me about touring Europe with a band and about his psychiatrist in Massachusetts. Simon sits beside him. He is very young, and wears a torn polyester jacket, which is zipped to his chin. He stares past me, to a frieze of Jesus in the Garden of Gethsemane, as he pulls apart Empire biscuits and arranges the glacé cherries in glossy patterns on his tray.

Archie is a recovering alcoholic in his late forties. He wears an immaculate pale blue shirt with a cutaway collar – donated by the Sue Ryder charity, he tells me, "but originally designed by Tom Ford". The table becomes quiet as he begins to talk about his drinking, and the incarceration that always followed.

"I didn't know about work," Archie says, through genuine bewilderment, rather than by way of excuse. "I thought that when you hit a certain age, you went and stood in the pub. You all just stood in the pub with your mates. And the very few times you weren't there, you were talking about what it was like being there. Or you were looking for a reason to go."

For a moment, Archie squares his broad shoulders and feigns aggression. John says nothing; Simon wheezes, as his eyelids close, and he inhales butane gas through the sleeve of his shirt. Slowly, his eyelids flutter, and his fingers begin to wriggle in the pockets of his coat.

"I never had a good start in life, going in and out of kiddies' homes," Archie continues. "In fact, I'll tell you this," he says, "I've seen a hell of a sight more violence in kiddies' homes than I ever have in prisons. And I've been on landings with lifers." Suddenly, he stands up, and his chair falls backward, screeching as it hits the floor.

Addiction marks people with all the force of a hatchet, or a sculptor's chisel; it carves contours in haunted faces, and tears seams in weathered skin. The men who come to Magdalene House have little interest in food, or warmth or company. They are weary, tortured, ghosts of people – with bodies contorted by imperceptible pain.

When I walk across Edinburgh to meet Archie's friend Jack, work on the skyline has stalled. At the top of Leith Walk, they've torn down the tenements, and the abandoned diggers and cement mixers look other-worldly. A rusted wrecking ball swings like a bauble above a chasm in the city where a thousand people used to live and breathe.

Greenside Place is a stretch of grubby pavement in front of a quiet cinema complex beside one of central Edinburgh's busiest roundabouts. As I traipse up Leith Walk, my eyes grow used to the darkness – and I can make out the street people, who seem drawn like ragged moths to the light.

Jack is a gentle older man with shorn gray hair and intense blue eyes. He wears a pair of dark jeans and a red sweatshirt that says "Nebraska". He has a very soft Northern accent, an occasional stammer, and a tendency to apologise. His fingernails are broken, and there's a hard, white groove where he once wore a wedding band, pressed like twine into pork fat on his right hand.

At first, we say very little, but eventually Jack mutters,

"Suppose you're sitting in a bedsit over there, and you're on your own, and you've only got a little TV. If you've got a hundred pounds in your pocket, and you go out on a Friday night, put a nice shirt on." He pauses. "Maybe put your hair up and put on a nice dress if you're a girl. If you go out clubbing then you're the same as the next man. You're a millionaire for a night."

Jack takes a plastic lighter from his pocket and taps it on the table.

"A lot of it's in the mind. Alcoholism is, because alcohol, if you only do it every now and again, it will lift you. Boom," he says, for emphasis, making the shape of gun in a gesture that feels unfortunate and sudden, and his eyes narrow. "But if you're doing it continuously, what alcohol will do is it will bring you up, and then it'll bring you right back down."

Jack hits his left palm off his right hand, and the resulting crack echoes like a gunshot.

"You won't get the up again because you're just on a continuous roll with it. That's the difference."

Extract from *Stone Cold* by Robert Swindells

In this extract from the novel *Stone Cold*, which was first published in 1993, the narrator Link describes his experience of sleeping rough on the streets.

If you think sleeping rough's just a matter of finding a dry spot where the **fuzz** won't move you on and getting your head down, you're wrong. Not your fault of course – if you've never tried it you've no way of knowing what it's like, so what I thought I'd do was sort of talk you through a typical night. That night in the Vaudeville alcove won't do, because there were two of us and it's worse if you're by yourself.

So you pick your spot. Wherever it is (unless you're in a squat or a derelict house or something) it's going to have a floor of stone, tile, concrete or brick. In other words it's going to be hard and cold. It might be a bit cramped, too – shop doorways often are. And remember, if it's winter you're going to be half frozen before you even start. Anyway you've got your place, and if you're lucky enough to have a sleeping bag you unroll it and get in.

Settled for the night? Well maybe, maybe not. Remember my first night? The Scouser? 'Course you do. He kicked me out of my bedroom and pinched my watch. Well, that sort of thing can happen any night, and there are worse things. You could be peed on by a drunk or a dog. Happens all the time – one man's bedroom is another man's lavatory. You might be spotted by a gang of lager louts on the look out for someone to maim. That happens all the time too, and if they get carried away you can end up dead. There are the guys who like young boys, who think because you're a dosser you'll do anything for dosh, and there's the psycho who'll knife you for your pack.

So, you lie listening. You bet you do. Footsteps. Voices. Breathing, even. Doesn't help you sleep.

Then there's your bruises. What bruises? Try lying on a stone floor for half an hour. Just half an hour. You can choose any position you fancy, and you can change position as often as you like. You won't find it comfy, I can tell you. You won't sleep unless you're dead drunk or zonked on downers. And if you are, and do, you're going to wake up with bruises on hips, shoulders, elbows, ankles and knees – especially if you're a bit thin from not eating properly. And if you do that six hours a night for six nights you'll feel like you fell out of a train. Try sleeping on concrete then.

And don't forget the cold. If you've ever tried dropping

off to sleep with cold feet, even in bed, you'll know it's impossible. You've got to warm up those feet, or lie awake. And in January, in a doorway, in wet trainers, it can be quite a struggle. And if you manage it, chances are you'll need to get up for a pee, and then it starts all over again.

And those are only some of the hassles. I haven't mentioned stomach cramps from hunger, headaches from the flu, toothache, fleas and lice. I haven't talked about homesickness, depression or despair. I haven't gone into how it feels to want a girlfriend when your circumstances make it virtually impossible for you to get one – how it feels to know you're a social outcast in fact, a non-person to whom every ordinary everyday activity is closed.

So. You lie on your bruises, listening. Trying to warm your feet. You curl up on your side and your hip hurts, so you stretch out on your back so your feet stay cold and the concrete hurts your heels. You force yourself to lie still for a bit, thinking that'll help you drop off, but it doesn't. Your pack feels like a rock under your head and your nose is cold. You wonder what time it is. Can you stop listening now, or could someone still come? Distant chimes. You strain your ears, counting. One o'clock? It can't be only one o'clock, surely? I've been here hours. Did I miss a chime?

What's that? Sounds like breathing. Heavy breathing,

as in maniac. Lie still. Quiet. Maybe he won't see you. Listen. Is he still there? Silence now. Creeping up, perhaps. No. Relax. Jeez, my feet are cold.

fuzz police

Extract from *Some Country Houses and their Owners* by James Lees-Milne

The National Trust is a charity which preserves historic houses and landscapes. In the 1930s and 1940s, James Lees-Milne visited country houses and estates across the country to persuade their aristocratic owners to donate their homes to the National Trust. Here, he describes his visit to Ham House in Richmond, Surrey on the 19th March 1943.

This afternoon I took the tube to Richmond, and thence a bus to Petersham. I walked down the long drive to Ham House. The grounds are indescribably overgrown and unkempt. I walked round the house, which appeared thoroughly deserted, searching for an entrance. The garden and front doors looked as though they had not been used for decades. So I returned to the back door and pulled a bell. Several seconds later a rusty tinkling echoed from distant subterranean regions. While waiting I recalled the grand ball given for Nefertiti Bethell which I attended in this house some ten years ago or more. The door was roughly jerked open, the bottom grating against the stone floor. The noise was accompanied by heavy breathing from within. An elderly man of sixty stood before me. He had red hair and a red face, carrot and port wine. He wore a tail coat and a starched shirt front which had come apart from the waistcoat. 'The old alcoholic family butler,' I said to myself. Without asking my name or business, he said, 'Follow me.' Slowly he led me down a dark passage, his legs moving in painful jerks. At last he stopped outside a door, and knocked nervously. An ancient voice cried, 'Come in!' The seedy butler then said to me, 'Daddy is expecting you,' and left me. I realized that he was the bachelor son of Sir Lyonel Tollemache, aged eighty-nine. As I entered the ancient voice said, 'You can leave us alone, boy!'

Sir Lyonel was sitting on an upright chair. He was dressed, unlike his son, immaculately in a grey suit, beautifully pressed, and wore a stock tie with a large pearl pin. I think he had **spats** over black polished shoes. A decorative figure, and courteous. He asked me several questions about the National Trust's scheme for preserving country houses, before ringing the bell and handing me back to his son.

The son showed me hurriedly round the house, which is melancholy in the extreme. All the rooms are dirty and dusty. The furniture and pictures have been moved to the country for safety. There is no doubt whatever that, even without the contents, this house is worthy of acceptance because of the superlative interior treatment, the panelling, the exquisite parquetry floors, the extraordinary chimneypieces, the great staircase of pierced **balusters**, the velvet hangings, etc. It is a wonderful seventeenth-century house, and from the south windows the garden layout of symmetrical beds, stone gate plinths and ironwork is superb. Once we were away from the father, whom whom he clearly holds in mortal dread, the son became confidential. He said the family were worth £2 million and did not receive as much as sixpence in each pound; that they had two gardeners instead of twelve, and no indoor servants except a cook (and himself). He told me he was so distracted by looking after the Ham property and the Lincolnshire estate that at times he felt suicidal. I looked straight at him, and knew that the poor man meant it. When I waved goodbye, the faintest flicker of a smile crossed his **bucolic** face, and a tiny tear was on his cheek.

---

spats a footwear accessory that covers the ankle
balusters a staircase railing
bucolic to do with country life

Extract from *Past Imperfect* by Julian Fellowes

I did know that Damian had done well, though how or why I knew I cannot now remember, for we shared no pals and moved in completely different circles. I must have seen his name on a *Sunday Times* list or maybe in an article on a financial page. But I don't think, before that evening, I understood quite *how* well he had done. We sped through the Surrey lanes and it was soon clear, from the trimmed hedging and the pointed walls, from the lawns like billiard tables and the glistening, weeded gravel, that we had entered the Kingdom of the Rich. Here there were no crumbling gate piers, no empty stables and lodges with leaking roofs. This was not a question of tradition and former glory. I was witnessing not the memory but the living presence of money.

I do have some experience of it. As a moderately successful writer, one rubs up against what Nanny would call 'all sorts,' but I can't pretend this was ever really my crowd. Most of the so-called rich I know are possessed of surviving, not newborn, fortunes, the rich who used to be a good deal richer. But the houses I was passing belonged to the Now Rich, which is different, and for me there is something invigorating in their sense of immediate power. It is peculiar, but even today there is a snobbery in Britain when it comes to new money. The traditional Right might be expected to turn up their noses at it I suppose, but paradoxically, it is often the intellectual Left who advertise their disapproval of the self-made. I do not pretend to understand how this is compatible with a belief in equality of opportunity. Perhaps they do not try to synthesise them, but just live by contradictory impulses, which I suppose we all do to some degree. But if I may have been guilty of such unimaginative thinking in my youth, it is gone from me now. These days I unashamedly admire men and women who have made their pile, just as I admire anyone who looks at the future mapped out for them at birth and is not afraid to tear it up and draw a better one. The self-made have more chance than most of finding a life that truly suits. I salute them for it and I salute their bejewelled world. Of course, on a personal level it was extremely annoying that Damian Baxter should be a part of it.

The house he had chosen as a setting for his splendour was not a fallen nobleman's palace but rather one of those self-consciously moral, Arts and Crafts, rambling warrens that seem to belong in a Disney cartoon and are no more convincing as a symbol of Olde England than they were when Lutyens built them at the turn of the last century. Surrounding it were gardens, terraced, clipped and criss-crossed with trim and tended paths, but seemingly no land beyond that. Damian had not apparently decided to adopt the ancient model of imitation gentry. This was not a manor house, nestling in the warm embrace of farming acres. This was simply the home of a Great Success.

Having said that, while not traditional in an aristocratic sense, the whole thing had quite a 1930s feel, as if it were built with the ill-gotten gains of a **First World War profiteer**. The Agatha Christie element provided by the chauffeur was continued by the bowing butler at the door and even by a housemaid, glimpsed on my way to the pale oak staircase, in her black dress and frilly apron, although she seemed perhaps more frivolous, as if I had suddenly been transported to the set of a Gershwin musical. A sense of the odd unreality of the adventure was, if anything, confirmed when I was shown to my room without first having met my host. There is always a slight whodunnit shiver of danger in this arrangement. A dark-clad servant hovering in the door and muttering 'Please come down to the drawing room when you are ready, Sir,' seems more suited to the reading of a will than a social call. But the room itself was nice enough. It was lined with pale-blue damask, which had also been used to drape the high, four-poster bed. The furniture was stable, solid English stuff and a group of **Chinoiserie** paintings on glass, between the windows, was really charming, even if there was the unmistakable tinge of a country house hotel, rather than a real country house, about it all, confirmed by the bathroom, which was sensational, with a huge bath, a walk-in shower, shiny taps on tall pipes coming straight up out of the floor, and enormous towels, fluffy and brand new. As we know, this kind of detail is seldom found in private houses in the shires, even today. I tidied myself up and went downstairs.

The drawing room was predictably cavernous, with a vaulted ceiling and those over-springy carpets that have been too recently replaced. Not the shagpile of the minted club owner, nor the flat and ancient rugs of the posh, but smooth and sprung and *new*. Everything in the room had been purchased within living memory and apparently by a single purchaser. There was none of the ragbag of tastes that country houses are inclined to represent, where the contents of a dozen homes, the amalgamated product of forty amateur collectors over two or three centuries are flung together into a single room. But it was good. In fact, it was excellent, the furniture largely from the early years of the eighteenth century, the pictures rather later, all fine, all shining clean and all in tip-top condition. After the similar experience of my bedroom, I wondered if Damian had employed a buyer, someone whose job was just to put his life together. Either way, there was no very tangible sense of him, or any other personality really, in the room. I wondered about, glancing at the paintings, unsure whether to stand or sit. In truth it felt forlorn, despite its splendour; the burning coals in the grate could not dispel the slightly clammy atmosphere, as if the room had been cleaned but not used for quite a while. And there were no flowers, which I always think a telltale sign; there was nothing living, in fact, giving a staleness to its perfection, a kind of lifeless sterility. I could not imagine what a woman had played much part in its creation, nor, God knows, that a child had played any part at all.

There was a sound at the door. 'My dear chap,' said a voice, still with the slight hesitance, the suspicion of a stammer, that I remembered so well. 'I hope I haven't kept you waiting.'

First World War profiteer someone who profited from the First World War, e.g. by selling weapons etc.
Chinoiserie a style of art characterized by the use of Chinese motifs

Newspaper article about the 'super rich'

The following extract is a newspaper article which was published in *The Independent* on the 20th October 2015 and describes the problems faced by the super rich.

A new breed of 'wealth therapists' is here to help the super rich

Lonely, troubled by guilt and loathed by Occupy activists – it can be tough being one of the 1 per cent.

Imagine, for a moment, that you are a member of the super-rich, one of the fabled 1 per cent, that exclusive club that has more money than the rest of us put together. Lucky you. You exist on a plane where whim is the reason you get out of bed each morning: the purchase of a tropical island, the acquisition of more gold taps for your bathroom. Your wardrobe – which is walk-in, naturally – might even boast more Jimmy Choos than Victoria Beckham's (also walk-in). The 99 per cent **languish** beneath you in perpetual soft-focused **toil** and struggle, and life is good, right?

Wrong. In 2015, you, hypothetical moneybags, have been bestowed with a conscience, and your bank balance is starting to feel like a burden. You need help. (You can afford it.) Your condition even has its own name now: wealth fatigue syndrome. And there are an increasing number of specialist therapists on hand to help, and from whom you will receive what you likely won't from the rest of society: a sympathetic ear.

"The media's idea of the 1 per cent is people that go out all the time and party, and buy cars, and keep spending," says Jamie Traeger-Muney, an American psychologist practising in Israel, and the founder of the Wealth Legacy Group, which aims to help the wealthy "lead a rich life". "But my clients have more sense of conflict over their wealth. They feel lucky and privileged, yes, but they also have unique problems to deal with, and my work is to make them feel more comfortable with their status, to help them see what positive changes they can make in their lives."

Many such millionaires, she suggests, struggle with the safety nets into which they were born – and statistics show that most were indeed born into wealth; few make it themselves. They often go to great lengths to conceal their fortune in social circles in an attempt to pass themselves off as "normal". "There is a lot of secrecy around wealth, especially with friends," she says, suggesting that many are scared to "come out" if they are the kind of person that cannot just foot the bill in any restaurant they visit, but buy the restaurant, too.

In New York, a therapist called Clay Cockrell has a growing speciality in the problems of the **über** wealthy. His clients range from those with a couple of million in the bank, to those that could buy France, and still have change for Belgium. What unifies them, he says, "is a certain amount of guilt about it. And they often face very serious problems: isolation, a lack of motivation" – the very problems revealed by the billionaire Minecraft designer Markus Persson in a series of tweets last summer. Another problem, says Cockrell, is how to raise children in such an environment. One need only look at the world of celebrity – hello Justin Bieber – to see that living within a world of **perpetual whim** and privilege is no guarantee for perpetual happiness."It is natural for parents to want to protect their children and to not have hardships, but they forget that struggle builds character and gives you perseverance, grit, determination. When they don't have that, they become spoilt."

So what is the solution? Bill Gates would suggest excessive **philanthropy**, while many a hip-hop impresario seems quite happy building entertainment empires and funding youth projects. But still there is struggle. Mo' money, as the sage put it (specifically, in this case, Biggie Smalls), mo' problems.

"In the past 50 years, we have gone from spending

almost all of our income on food and shelter, to having all this extra money to do all sorts of things with," says Dr Bernard Burchell, a reader at the University of Cambridge's sociology department. And so while our knee-jerk reaction is to resent the rich, we also desperately **covet** their fortunes.

"Money equates to status," Dr Burchell adds, "which is why we get so concerned about our pay rises each year, especially when our colleagues might get a little more than us. It's a subject that endlessly obsesses us."

And so we will continue to demonise the 1 per cent, which is easy – and, whisper it, fun – to do as long as we keep two-dimensionalising them. But as Jamie Traeger-Muney points out, the rich are people, too.

"This isn't a request to the world to please, boo-hoo, feel sorry for the wealthy," she says. "Therapy is just a way to provide a safe place for them to have a conversation to help them figure things out. And at the end of the day, we all deserve that, right?"

---

languish live in miserable conditions
toil hard work
über extremely
perpetual continual
whim a sudden desire or change of mind
philanthropy concern for your fellow human beings, especially as shown by kind and generous acts that benefit large numbers of people
covet to wish to have something that belongs to someone else

Sport and entertainment

The 20th and 21st centuries saw an increase in the time people had available to spend on leisure activities. From attending football matches to visits to the cinema or the concert hall, sport and entertainment filled the time that people had off from their working lives.

From the school field to the stadium, football is the most popular sport in Britain, whilst the Olympic Games is often seen as the pinnacle of sporting achievement with athletes training hard to attain an elusive gold medal. The texts in this section explore the challenges and appeal of these and other sports.

In the field of entertainment, music and cinema became multibillion pound industries in the 20th century. In the 1960s the Beatles emerged from Liverpool to become a global phenomenon, whilst cinema-going became a popular leisure activity.

Extract from *The Meaning of Sport* by Simon Barnes

> The following extract is taken from *The Meaning of Sport*, which was first published in 2006. Here, the sports writer Simon Barnes explores the qualities required by an Olympic athlete.

If David Beckham had been an Olympian he would be seen as a waster. Or at least, as a man who missed his destiny. A man who failed to seize his time. And that is the art of being an Olympian: the seizing of the time. The great beauty, the great perfection of an Olympian is that he or she must perform in the knowledge that there is no second chance.

The Olympic Games is, as I have said, often compared with the World Cup. This is not a sensible comparison. Beckham failed at the World Cup in 1998. He kicked an Argentinian, got sent off, England lost, and were out of the competition. Beckham became a national hate-object as a result. And there was not another World Cup for four years, so **redemption** would have been a very long way away if the World Cup was the only prize in football worth playing for.

But that is the way it always is for an Olympian – someone who takes part in one of the heartland Olympic sports, like athletics, swimming, rowing, gymnastics, sports for which nothing matters – nothing matters at all – except the Olympic Games. If you fail at the Olympic Games you have nothing. Nothing for four years. And that is what gives the Games that extraordinary intensity. Winning is not just about being perfect. It is about being perfect now. The unforgiving present tense of the Olympic Games dominates the hearts and minds of the competitors. If not now, when?

For Beckham, there was redemption to be found as soon as the following year. Consequently, he was able to perform one of the great self-rescuing acts in the history of sport. He refused to leave the country, as many recommended. Instead, he stayed with Manchester United and inspired them to their immortal treble of the 1998–99 season: the Premiership, FA Cup and European Cup.

But for an Olympian, there are no consolation prizes, and, if you seek a second chance, you must wait nearly half a sporting lifetime for it. And very few athletes in any discipline have eight years at the top. If you mess up the Olympic Games, you have four years for the suffering. In Atlanta 1996, Paula Radcliffe finished fifth in the 5,000 metres. In Sydney at the 2000 Olympic Games, Radcliffe led most of the way in the 10,000 metres and finished fourth. She then reinvented herself as a marathon runner, and set some astonishing world records. But this is athletics, a heartland Olympic sport, and so naturally Radcliffe still hungered for the sport's ultimate reward. She wanted an Olympic gold medal. And this was her time. It was hers for the seizing.

The greatest seizer of them all was Steve Redgrave. I saw him win his fifth gold medal at his fifth Olympic Games in Sydney; and it will go down at the greatest piece of sport I have ever seen. I am not challenging for originality here: it was the greatest piece of sport anybody has ever seen. **Longevity**, it seems to me, is an **ineluctable** aspect of sporting greatness.

I was also at the waterside in 2004 to see Matthew Pinsent claim his fourth gold medal. And it was as fine an example of time-seizing as you could ever wish to see. There was something gloriously mythical about it: an echo of the *Odyssey*, the story of a ship cursed by the gods. The hero prevails in the end, after many **tribulations** and, at last, he can pause and weep an ocean of tears: just as Pinsent did.

Pinsent's boat had originally been a pair, which won everything and then inexplicably failed. They finished fourth at the World Championship of 2003. The pair was sacked, and remade as a four. It didn't work. A man was dropped. Another was injured. And then eight weeks before the Games, another member, Alex Partridge, suffered a collapsed lung and dropped out. Ed Coode came back into the four: seven weeks. An Olympic crew normally takes four years to create.

It was terrifyingly close. The British crew went side-by-side with Canada from start to finish and throughout, Canada held the slightest advantage. It was perfectly clear that this was a heroic British effort doomed to end in failure. There was a feeling of glum inevitability about the process: a feeling that your best is never, ever quite good enough, not for the things you really want. But, impossibly, the British four won in the last ten strokes, and they did so because of Pinsent. He recalls thinking: 'We're doing our best and we're still not making any inroads at all.' Desperate times require desperate measures. Great times require great people to seize them. Pinsent took the crew over the line by means of a massive outpouring of the self. He refused to accept the plain and obvious fact of defeat, and remade reality in front of us. It was one of the most stirring pieces of sport I have ever witnessed.

---

redemption making up for doing badly in the past
longevity long life
ineluctable inescapable
tribulations great troubles or hardships

Extract from *A Kestrel for a Knave* by Barry Hines

FICTION

The following extract is taken from the novel *A Kestrel for a Knave*, which was first published in 1968. Here, Billy Caspar is waiting to be picked for a game of football, organized by his P.E. teacher, Mr Sugden.

They lined up, jumping and running on the spot, those with long sleeves clutching the cuffs in their hands, those without massaging their goosey arms.

'Tibbut, come out here and be the other captain.'

Tibbut walked out and stood facing the line, away from Mr Sugden.

'I'll have first pick, Tibbut.'

'That's not right, Sir.'

'Why isn't it?'

''Cos you'll get all the best players.'

'Rubbish, lad.'

'Course you will, Sir. It's not fair.'

'Tibbut. Do you want to play football? Or do you want to get dressed and go and do some maths?'

'Play football, Sir.'

'Right then, stop moaning and start picking. I'll have Anderson.'

He turned away from Tibbut and pointed to a boy who was standing on one of the intersections of the centre circle and the half-way line. Anderson walked off this cross and stood behind him. Tibbut scanned the line, considering his choice.

'I'll have Purdey.'

'Come on then, Ellis.'

Each selection altered the structure of the line. When Tibbut had been removed from the centre, all the boys sidestepped to fill the gap. The same happened when Anderson went from near one end. But when Purdey and Ellis, who had been standing side by side, were removed, the boys at their shoulders stood still, therefore dividing the original line into two. These new lines were swiftly segmented as more boys were chosen, leaving no trace of the first major division, just half a dozen boys looking across spaces at each other, reading from left to right, a fat boy; an arm's length away, two friends, one tall with glasses, the other short with a hare-lip; then a space of two yards and Billy; a boy space away from him, a thin boy with a crew-cut and a spotty face, and right away from these, at the far end of the line, another fat boy. Spotty Crew-Cut was half-way between the two fat boys, therefore half of the length of the line was occupied by five of the boys. The far fat boy was the next to go, which halved the length of the line and left Spotty Crew-Cut as one of the end markers.

Tibbut then selected the tall friend with glasses, Mr Sugden immediately selected his partner. They separated gradually as they walked away from the line, parting finally to enter their respective teams. And then there were three: Fatty, Billy, and Spotty Crew-Cut, blushing across at each other while the captains considered. Tibbut picked Crew-Cut. He dashed forward into the anonymity of his team. Fatty stood grinning. Billy stared down at the earth. After long deliberation Mr Sugden chose Billy, leaving Tibbut with Hobson's choice; but before either Billy or Fatty could move towards their teams, Mr Sugden was already turning away and shouting instructions.

'Right! We'll play down hill!'

The team broke for their appropriate halves, and while they were arguing their claims for positions, Mr Sugden jogged to sideline, dropped the ball, and took off his tracksuit. Underneath he was wearing a crisp red football shirt with white cuffs and a white band round the neck. A big white 9 filled most of the back, whiter than his white nylon shorts, which showed a slight fleshy tint through the material. He pulled his socks up, straightened the ribs, then took a fresh roll of half inch bandage from his tracksuit and ripped off two lengths. The torn bandage packet, the cup of its structure still intact, blew away over the turf like the damaged shell of a dark blue egg. Mr Sugden used the lengths of bandage to secure his stockings just below the knees, then he folded his tracksuit neatly on the ground, looked down at himself, and walked on to the pitch carrying the ball like a plum pudding on the tray of his hand. Tibbut, standing on the centre circle, with his hands down his shorts, winked at his Left Winger and waiting for Mr Sugden to approach.

'Who are you today, Sir, Liverpool?'

'Rubbish, lad! Don't you know your club colours yet?'

'Liverpool are red, aren't they, Sir?'

'Yes, but they're all red, shirts, shorts and stockings. These are Manchester United's colours.'

''Course they are, Sir, I forgot. What position are you playing?'

Mr Sugden turned his back on him to show him the number 9.

'Bobby Charlton. I thought you were usually Denis Law when you were Manchester United.'

'It's too cold to play as a striker today. I'm scheming this morning, all over the field like Charlton.'

'Law plays all over, Sir. He's not only a striker.'

'He doesn't link like Charlton.'

'Better player though, Sir.'

Sugden shook his head. 'No, he's been badly off form recently.'

'Makes no odds, he's still a better player. He can settle a game in two minutes.'

'Are you trying to tell *me* about football, Tibbut?'

'No, Sir.'

'Well shut up then. Anyway Law's in the wash this week.'

He placed the ball on the centre spot and looked round at his team. There was only Billy out of position. He was standing between the full backs, the three of them forming a domino : : : pattern with the half backs. The goal was empty. Mr Sugden pointed at it.

'There's no one in goal!'

His team looked round to confirm this observation, but Tibbut's team had beaten them to it by just looking straight ahead.

'Casper! What position are supposed to be playing?'

Billy looked to the Right Back, the Left Back, the Right Back again. Neither of them supplied the answer, so he answered the question himself.

'I don't know, Sir. Inside Right?'

This answer made 1: Mr Sugden angry. 2: the boys laugh.

'Don't talk ridiculous, lad! How can you be playing Inside Right back there?'

He looked up at the sky.

'God help us; fifteen years old and still doesn't know the positions of a football team!'

He levelled one arm at Billy.

'Get in goal, lad!'

'O, Sir! I can't goal. I'm no good.'

'Now's your chance to learn then, isn't it?'

'I'm fed up o' goin' in goal. I go in every week.'

Billy turned round and looked at the goal as though it was the portal leading into the gladiatorial arena.

'Don't stand looking, lad. Get in there!'

'Well don't blame me then, when I let 'em all through.'

'Of course I'll blame you, lad! Who do you expect me to blame?'

Billy cursed him quietly all the way back to the nets.

Extract from *Brighton Rock* by Graham Greene

The following extract is taken from the novel *Brighton Rock*, which was first published in 1938. Here, Greene describes the crowds gathering to watch the horse-racing.

A band came up the pavement through **Old Steyne**, a blind band playing drums and trumpets, walking in the gutter, feeling the kerb with the edge of their shoes, in Indian file. You heard the music a long way off, persisting through the rumble of the crowd, the shots of exhaust pipes, and the grinding of the buses starting uphill for the racecourse. It rang out with spirit, marched like a regiment, and you raised your eyes in expectation of the tiger skin and the twirling drumsticks and saw the pale blind eyes, like those of pit ponies, going by along the gutter.

In the public school grounds above the sea the girls trooped solemnly out to hockey: stout goal-keepers padded like armadillos; captains discussing tactics with their lieutenants; junior girls running amok in the bright day. Beyond the aristocratic turf, through the wrought-iron main gates they could see the **plebeian** procession, those whom the buses wouldn't hold, plodding up the down, kicking up the dust, eating buns out of paper bags. The buses took the long way round through **Kemp Town**, but up the steep hill came the crammed taxicabs – a seat for anyone at ninepence a time – a **Packard** for the members' enclosure, old **Morrises**, strange high cars with family parties, keeping the road after twenty years. It was as if the whole road moved upwards like an Underground staircase in the dusty sunlight, a creaking, shouting, jostling crowd of cars moving with it. The junior girls took to their heels like ponies racing on the turf, feeling the excitement going on outside, as if this were a day on which life for many people reached a kind of climax. The odds on Black Boy had shortened, nothing could ever make life quite the same after that rash bet of a fiver on Merry Monarch. A scarlet racing model, a tiny **rakish** car which carried about it the atmosphere of **innumerable roadhouses**, of **totsies** gathered round swimming pools, of furtive encounters in by-lanes off the Great North Road, wormed through the traffic with incredible dexterity. The sun caught it: it winked as far as the dining-hall windows of the girls' school. It was crammed tight: a woman sat on a man's knee, and another man clung on the running board as it swayed and hooted and cut in and out uphill towards the **downs**. The woman was singing, her voice faint and disjointed through the horns, something traditional about brides and bouquets, something which went with Guinness and oysters and the old Leicester Lounge, something out of place in the little bright racing car. Upon the top of the down the words blew back along the dusty road to meet an ancient Morris rocking and receding in their wake at forty miles an hour, with flapping hood, bent fender and discoloured windscreen.

Old Steyne a thoroughfare in central Brighton
plebeian of or belonging to common people
Kemp Town an area of Brighton
Packard a type of luxury American car
Morris a type of car
rakish jaunty and dashing in appearance
innumerable too many to be counted
roadhouses pubs, bars
totsies attractive young women
downs the South Downs, the hills around Brighton

Extract from *Unreliable Memoirs* by Clive James

The following extract is taken from *Unreliable Memoirs*, the first volume of Clive James' autobiography which was first published in 1980. Here, James describes his childhood experience of visiting the cinema.

Every Saturday afternoon at the pictures there was a feature film, sixteen cartoons and an episode each from four different serials. The programme just went on and on like **Bayreuth**. The Margaret Street children would join up with the Irene Street children and the combined mass would add themselves unto the Sunbeam Avenue children and the aggregate would join the swarm from all the other areas all moving north along Rocky Point Road towards Rockdale, where the Odeon stood. In summer the concrete paths were hot. The asphalt footpaths were even hotter: bubbles of tar formed, to be squashed flat by our leathery bare feet. Running around on **macadamised** playgrounds throughout the spring, by summer we had feet that could tread on a drawing pin and hardly feel it.

When you got to the Odeon the first thing you did was stock up with lollies. Lollies was the word for what the English call sweets and the Americans call candy. Some of the more privileged children had upwards of five shillings each to dispose of, but in fact two bob was enough to buy you as much as you could eat. Everyone, without exception, bought at least one Hoadley's Violet Crumble Bar. It was a slab of dense, dry honeycomb coated with chocolate. So frangible was the honeycomb that it would shatter when bitten, scattering bright yellow shrapnel. It was like trying to eat a Ming vase. The honeycomb would go soft only after a day's exposure to direct sunlight. The chocolate surrounding it, however, would liquefy after only ten minutes in a dark cinema.

Fantails came in a weird, blue, rhomboidal packet shaped like an isosceles triangle with one corner missing. Each individual Fantail was wrapped in a piece of paper detailing a film star's biography – hence the pun, fan tales. The Fantail itself was a chocolate-coated toffee so glutinous that it could induce lockjaw in a mule. People had to have their mouths chipped open with a cold chisel. One packet of Fantails would last an average human being for ever. A group of six small boys could go through a packet during the course of a single afternoon at the pictures, but it took hard work and involved a lot of strangled crying in the dark. Any fillings you had in your second teeth would be removed instantly, while children who still had any first teeth left didn't keep them long.

The star lolly, outstripping even the Violet Crumble

Bar and the Fantail in popularity, was undoubtedly the Jaffa. A packet of Jaffas was loaded like a cluster bomb with about fifty globular lollies the size of ordinary marbles. The Jaffa had a dark chocolate core and a brittle orange candy coat: in cross section it looked rather like the planet Earth. It presented two alternative ways of being eaten, each with its allure. You could fondle the Jaffa on the tongue until your saliva ate its way through the casing, whereupon the taste of chocolate would invade your mouth with a sublime, majestic inevitability. Or you could bite straight through and submit the interior of your head to a stunning explosion of flavour. Sucking and biting your way through forty or so Jaffas while Jungle Jim wrestled with the crocodiles, you nearly always had a few left over after the stomach could take no more. The spare Jaffas made ideal ammunition. Flying through the dark, they would bounce off an infantile skull with the noise of bullets hitting a bell. They showered on the stage when the manager came out to announce the lucky ticket. The Jaffa is a part of Australia's theatrical heritage. There was a famous occasion, during the Borovansky Ballet production of *Giselle* at the Tivoli in Sydney, when **Albrecht** was forced to abandon the performance. It was a special afternoon presentation of the ballet before an audience of schoolchildren. Lying in a swoon while awaiting the reappearance of Giselle, Albrecht aroused much comment because of his **protuberant codpiece**.

118

After being hit square on the power-bulge by a speeding Jaffa, he woke up with a rush and hopped off the stage in the stork position.

Bayreuth an opera festival
macadamised covered in tarmac
Albrecht a character in the opera *Giselle*
protuberant bulging out
codpiece a pouch that covers the crotch

Newspaper report about 'Beatlemania'

In the 1960s, the Beatles became the most popular group on the planet, causing mass hysteria wherever they appeared. The following extract is a newspaper report, written by the journalist Hella Pick and published in *The Guardian* on the 8th February 1964, describing the Beatles' first visit to the United States.

Beatle hysteria hits US

"After all the **lend-lease** we sent to Britain, did they have to do this to us?" Such was the comment of a distinctly square member of the New York community today after hearing of the Beatles' arrival. But there are not many **squares** in New York today.

Physically, the Beatle invasion was launched just after 1 p.m. when their air liner touched down to pandemonium at Kennedy Airport. But in fact New York has been in the tightening grip of Beatlemania for some weeks and the arrival merely confirmed that the idols really do exist in body as well as voice.

There were more than three thousand teenagers at the airport who had rallied from distant states as well as New York City, had skipped school, faced dismissal from their jobs, and were carrying placards that had such amorous slogans as "I love you, please stay." Just as there had been weeping when they left London, so there was weeping when the Beatles arrived here. But here the tears were for joy.

There were shouts too, and squeals when the four Beatles with their numerous entourage emerged from the plane. Maximum police protection had been called out for them – the kind of arrangement that is usually produced for Kings and Presidents. Certainly without the police barriers little would be left of the Beatles by now.

There will be a hundred policemen permanently with them while they are in the city – and one of the policemen drily remarked that the world had gone mad. He could not recall similar scenes since **General MacArthur** was recalled from Korea.

Today, radio stations from early morning had been playing Beatle records and yeah, yeah, yeah is on everybody's brain. Even **staid correspondents** were seen today doing their work to the Beatle rhythm, and in a supermarket the transistor was playing on a pile of oranges as the clerk packed up my purchases.

At my hairdressers, calls were pouring in from all manner of male hopefuls asking if their hair could be set in Beatle fashion, and Beatle wigs have been on sale for some time.

The Beatles have come here on a nationwide tour. Their first appearance will be on television on Sunday and an executive at the television network told me that they were swamped with firms demanding to sponsor the programme – that is have advertising time on them – while the Beatles perform. He said he almost felt like cutting his telephone wires to avoid further conversations about the Beatles.

The first live New York appearance will be of all places, in Carnegie Hall, that erstwhile stronghold of classical music – where every artist of international repute has sought to crown his achievement. Tickets were sold out within a few hours, and there is an inflated black market.

Millions of Beatle records have already been sold, and the best-selling Belgian nun with her gentle call to **Dominique** is nearly forgotten in the strident call to "Take her, she is mine."

---

lend-lease a US government policy supplying Britain with resources during the Second World War
square a slang term for a boring and out-of-touch person
General MacArthur an American general during the Korean War, who was greeted by scenes of adulation when he returned to the United States
staid respectable, unadventurous
correspondents journalists
Dominique a number one single by the Singing Nun

Extract from *Gig* by Simon Armitage

> The following extract is taken from *Gig*, a memoir by the
> poet Simon Armitage about his love of music. Here, he
> describes attending a concert by the Arctic Monkeys.

Not being able to get a ticket for Arctic Monkeys'
hometown gig for love nor money, I'm seeing them in
Leeds, at the university. I taught here for a while, in
the English Department, where the spectre of Geoffrey
Hill still walked the corridors. Geoffrey Hill – the only
living poet with a ghost. I don't believe Geoffrey is in
the audience tonight, either in body or in spirit, though it
would be hard to spot anyone in what seems to be a crowd
of several thousand in a venue designed for considerably
fewer. Most are students, which is a shame. I've got
nothing against them as a body of people, but students
at Leeds University tend to be from decent backgrounds
where nutritious foodstuffs were in plentiful supply,
which means they tend to be quite tall. So even at five
eleven (six foot in certain footwear and after a few drinks)
I'm going to struggle to see. Another problem with
tonight's undergraduate audience is that many of them

have never been to a gig before in their life, as evidenced by the way they're dressed. This isn't just about style; it's a question of practicability. A woman to my left is wearing a string of pearls. Her friend is wearing a ball gown. And anyone coming to a gig in a wooly jumper, a fleece or a toggled-up duffel coat, such as the guy about three rows in front of me, is either hoping to lose a lot of weight or is conducting a crude research project on self-combustion. Neither are tonight's audience particularly conversant with gig etiquette. One girl has brought a foldaway chair. One boy says 'Do you mind?' when he gets a bump from someone trying to pogo. On the plus side, it's good to see the lapel badge making a comeback, even if it is a badge pinned to the lapel of a pre-distressed jacket from Burton or decorating the epaulette of a combat shirt in desert camouflage colours from some celebrity designer's latest range of post-Gulf, military-chic fashionwear. Not that I'm in any position to poke fun at the middle classes. About ten years ago I came with a friend to see The Fall at the same venue. There were only a couple of hundred people in the crowd, including a cat, but we still managed to work up a sweat at the front. Afterwards, as people waited for buses in the rain at the top of Woodhouse Lane or set off walking into darkest Leeds, we hopped over the wall into the staff car park. 'You could take that T-shirt off and wring it out,' my friend said to me. I said, 'Doesn't matter, I've got a fresh one in the glove compartment.'

Arctic Monkeys were **catapulted** to prominence by demos and downloads, or so the story goes and without so much as a minute's airplay they were famous before anyone had heard of them. My friend Tony went to see them in Manchester a year ago and said they were going to be massive, and he wasn't wrong. He also said they'd brought a mob of their own followers with them – another bunch of people not familiar with gig etiquette – but not students this time. These were lads. A big gang of them. They were looking for trouble, and if they couldn't find it with the rest of the audience, they'd find it amongst themselves. Not nice, really. A disgrace, probably. But thankfully a useful number of them have breached campus security tonight and are giving it full whack at the front. It means that my definition of a good gig – more legs in the air than arms – is at least partially achieved. However, of all the things to rise above head height at a gig over the decades – hankies, flags, crowd-surfers, knickers, cigarette lighters and tape recorders – surely the least predictable was the camera-phone. It must be odd to be onstage, to lift your eyes away from your guitar for a moment and peer through your floppy fringe, only to be met by the gaze of a couple of hundred cyclopic Nokias and Samsungs and Sony Ericssons, all winking and flashing away.

---

catapulted launched, as if with a catapult

Crime and punishment

From newspaper front pages to the shelves of bestsellers in bookshops and libraries, crime has been a major concern in the 20th and 21st centuries. Gruesome murders have gripped the attention of the nation, whilst new technology has been used both to track down and capture criminals as well as inspiring new types of crime. However, behind the headlines, crime rates have been in decline in the 21st century, with experts proposing different theories for this drop in crime.

In the first half of the 20th century, anyone convicted of murder in Great Britain could still face the death penalty. After the death penalty was abolished in 1965, convicted murderers were instead sentenced to life imprisonment. For young people convicted of crimes such as robbery and assault, the harsh regime of borstal beckoned until these institutions were abolished in 1982.

Extract from *A Hanging*, an essay by George Orwell

In the 1920s, the writer George Orwell served in the British Imperial Police force in Burma (the country now known as Myanmar). In the following extract from an essay which was first published in 1931, Orwell describes the execution of a condemned criminal.

We set out for the gallows. Two warders marched on either side of the prisoner, with their rifles at the slope; two others marched close against him, gripping him by arm and shoulder, as though at once pushing and supporting him. The rest of us, magistrates and the like followed behind. Suddenly, when we had gone ten yards, the procession stopped short without any order or warning. A dreadful thing had happened – a dog, come goodness knows whence, had appeared in the yard. It came bounding among us with a loud volley of barks, and leapt round us wagging its whole body, wild with glee at finding so many human beings together. It was a large woolly dog, half **Airedale**, half **pariah**. For a moment it pranced round us, and then, before anyone could stop it, it had made a dash for the prisoner, and jumping up tried to lick his face. Everyone stood aghast, too taken aback even to grab at the dog.

'Who let that bloody brute in here?' said the superintendent angrily. 'Catch it, someone!'

A warder detached from the escort, charged clumsily after the dog, but it danced and gambolled just out of his reach, taking everything as part of the game. A young **Eurasian** jailer picked up a handful of gravel and tried to stone the dog away, but it dodged the stones and came after us again. Its yaps echoed from the jail walls. The prisoner, in the grasp of the two warders, looked on incuriously, as though this was another formality of the hanging. It was several minutes before someone managed to catch the dog. Then we put my handkerchief through its collar and moved off once more, with the dog still straining and whimpering.

It was about forty yards to the gallows. I watched the bare brown back of the prisoner marching in front of me. He walked clumsily with his bound arms, but quite steadily, with that bobbing gait of the Indian who never straightens his knees. At each step his muscles slid neatly into place, the lock of hair on his scalp danced up and down, his feet printed themselves on the wet gravel. And once, in spite of the men who gripped him by each shoulder, he stepped slightly aside to avoid a puddle on the path.

It is curious, but till that moment I had never realized

what it means to destroy a healthy, conscious man. When I saw the prisoner step aside to avoid the puddle. I saw the mystery, the unspeakable wrongness, of cutting a life short when it is in full time. This man was not dying, he was alive just as we are alive. All the organs of his body were working – bowels digesting food, skin renewing itself, nails growing, tissues forming – all toiling away in solemn foolery. His nails would still be growing when he stood on the drop, when he was falling through the air with a tenth-of-a-second to live. His eyes saw the yellow gravel and the grey walls, and his brain still remembered, foresaw, reasoned – reasoned even about puddles. He and we were a party of men walking together, seeing, hearing, feeling, understanding the same world; and in two minutes, with a sudden snap, one of us would be gone – one mind less, one world less.

Airedale a breed of dog
pariah a stray mongrel
Eurasian a person of mixed European and Asian ancestry

Extract from *The Loneliness of the Long Distance Runner* by Alan Sillitoe

> In the 20th century, children found guilty of crimes were often sent to borstal, an institution which aimed to discipline and educate young offenders. The following extract is taken from a short story, which was first published in 1959, about a teenage boy named Smith who is sent to borstal for robbing a bakery. Here, Smith describes his feelings about borstal.

I was nearly eighteen months in Borstal before I thought about getting out. I can't tell you much about what it was like there because I haven't got the hang of describing buildings or saying how many crumby chairs and slatted windows make a room. Neither can I do much complaining, because to tell you the truth I didn't suffer in Borstal at all. I gave the same answer a pal of mine gave when someone asked him how much he hated it in the army. "I didn't hate it," he said. "They fed me, gave me a suit, and pocket-money, which was a bloody sight more than I ever got before, unless I worked myself to death for it, and most of the time they wouldn't let me work but sent me to the dole office twice a week." Well, that's more or less what I say. Borstal didn't hurt me in that respect, so since I've got no complaints I don't have to describe what they gave us to eat, what the dorms were like, or how they treated us. But in another way Borstal does something to me. No, it doesn't get my back up, because it's always been up, right from when I was born. What it does do is show me what they've been trying to frighten me with. They've got other things as well, like prison and, in the end, **the rope**. It's like me rushing up to thump a man and snatch the coat off his back when, suddenly, I pull up because he whips out a knife and lifts it to stick me like a pig if I come too close. That knife is Borstal, **clink**, the rope. But once you've seen the knife you learn a bit of unarmed combat. You have to, because you'll never get that sort of knife in your own hands, and this unarmed combat doesn't amount to much. Still, there it is, and you keep on rushing up to this man, knife or not, hoping to get one of your hands on his wrist and the other on his elbow both at the same time, and press back until he drops the knife.

You see, by sending me to Borstal they've shown me the knife, and from now on I know something I didn't know before: that it's war between me and them. I always knew this, naturally, because I was in Remand Homes as well and the boys there told me a lot about their brothers in Borstal, but it was only touch and go then, like kittens, like boxing gloves, like dobbie. But now that they've shown me the knife, whether I ever pinch another thing in my life again or not, I know who my enemies are and what war is. They can drop all the atom bombs they like for all I care: I'll never call it war and wear a soldier's uniform, because I'm in a different sort of war, that they think is child's play. The war they think is war is suicide, and those that go and get skilled in war should be put in clink for attempted suicide because that's the feeling in blokes' minds when they rush to join up or let themselves be called up. I know, because I've thought how good it would be sometimes to do myself in and the easiest way to do it, it occurred to me, was to hope for a big war so's I could join up and get killed. But I got past that when I knew I already was in a war of my own, that I was born into one, that I grew up hearing the sound of 'old soldiers' who'd been over the top at Dartmoor, half-killed at Lincoln, trapped in no-man's-land at Borstal, that sounded louder than any **Jerry** bombs. Government wars aren't my wars; they've got **nowt** to do with me, because my own war's all that I'll ever be bothered about. I remember when I was fourteen and I went out into the country with three of my cousins, all about the same age, who later went to different Borstals, and then to different regiments, from which they soon deserted, and then to different **gaols** where they still are as far as I know.

But anyway, we were all kids then, and wanted to go

out to the woods for a change, to get away from the roads of stinking hot tar one summer. We climbed over fences and went through fields, **scrumping** a few sour apples on our way, until we saw the wood about a mile off. Up Colliers' Pad we heard another lot of kids talking in high-school voices behind a hedge. We crept up on them and peeped through the brambles, and saw they were eating a picnic, a real posh spread out of baskets and flasks and towels. There must have been about seven of them, lads and girls sent out by their mams and dads for the afternoon. So we went on our bellies through the hedge like crocodiles and surrounded them, and then dashed into the middle, scattering the fire and batting their tabs and snatching up all there was to eat, then running off over Cherry Orchard fields into the wood, with a man chasing us who'd come up while we were ransacking their picnic. We got away all right, and had a good feed into the bargain, because we'd been clambed to death and couldn't wait long enough to get our chops ripping into them thin lettuce and ham sandwiches and creamy cakes.

Well, I'll always feel during every bit of my life like those daft kids should have felt before we broke them up.

---

the rope hanging, capital punishment
clink prison
Jerry slang word for German used during the Second World War
nowt dialect word for nothing
gaols jails
scrumping stealing

Account of the arrest of
Dr Crippen

> In 1910, an accused murderer named Dr Crippen fled
> Britain with his accomplice, Ethel Le Neve, sailing for
> Canada on a ship named the *Montrose*. The captain of
> the ship, Captain Kendall, became suspicious and sent a
> wireless message, alerting the authorities to Dr Crippen's
> presence aboard the ship.

The *Montrose* was in port at Antwerp when I read in the
Continental Daily Mail that a warrant had been issued for
Crippen and le Neve. They were reported to have been
traced to a hotel in Brussels but had then vanished again.

Soon after we sailed for Quebec I happened to glance
through the porthole of my cabin and behind a lifeboat
I saw two men. One was squeezing the other's hand. I
walked along the boat deck and got into conversation
with the elder man. I noticed that there was a mark on
the bridge of his nose through wearing spectacles, that
he had recently shaved off a moustache, and that he was
growing a beard. The young fellow was very reserved,
and I remarked about his cough.

'Yes,' said the elder man, 'my boy has a weak chest,
and I'm taking him to California for his health.

I returned to my cabin and had another look at the *Daily Mail*. I studied the description and photographs issued by Scotland Yard. Crippen was 50 years of age, 5 ft 4 ins high, wearing spectacles and a moustache; Miss Le Neve was 27, 5 ft 5 ins, slim, with pale complexion. I then examined the passenger list and ascertained that the two passengers were travelling as 'Mr Robinson and son'. I arranged for them to take meals at my table.

When the bell went for lunch I tarried until the coast was clear, then slipped into the Robinsons' cabin unobserved, where I noticed two things: that the boy's felt hat was packed round the rim to make it fit, and that he had been using a piece of a woman's bodice as a face flannel. That satisfied me. I went down to the dining saloon and kept my eyes open. The boy's manners at table were ladylike. Later, when they were **promenading** the saloon deck, I went out and walked behind them, and called out, 'Mr Robinson!' I had to shout the name several times before the man turned and said to me, 'I'm sorry, Captain, I didn't hear you – this cold wind is making me deaf.'

In the next two days we developed our acquaintance. Mr Robinson was the **acme** of politeness, quiet-mannered, a non-smoker; at night he went on deck and roamed about on his own. Once the wind blew up his coat tails and in his hip pocket I saw a revolver. After that I also carried a revolver, and we often had pleasant little tea parties together in my cabin, discussing the book he was reading, which was *The Four Just Men*, a murder mystery by Edgar Wallace – and when that little fact was wirelessed to London and published it made Edgar Wallace's name ring, so **agog** was everybody in England over the Crippen case.

That brings me to the **wireless**. On the third day out I gave my wireless operator a message for Liverpool: *One hundred and thirty-miles west of Lizard . . . have strong suspicions that Crippen London cellar murderer and accomplice are among saloon passengers . . . Accomplice dressed as boy; voice, manner, and build undoubtedly a girl.*

I remember Mr Robinson sitting in a deckchair, looking at the wireless aerials and listening to the crackling of our crude spark-transmitter, and remarking to me what a wonderful invention it was.

I sent several more reports, but our weak transmitting apparatus was soon out of communication with land. We could hear other ships at a great distance, however, and you may imagine my excitement when my operator brought me a message he had intercepted from a London newspaper to its representative about the White Star liner *Laurentic* which was also heading westward across the Atlantic: *What is Inspector Dew doing? Is he sending and receiving wireless messages? Is he playing games with passengers? Are passengers excited over chase? Rush reply.*

This was the first I knew that my message to Liverpool

had caused Inspector Dew to catch the first boat out – the *Laurentic*. With her superior speed I knew she would reach the Newfoundland coast before me. I hoped that if she had any news for me the *Laurentic* would leave it at the Belle Island station to be transmitted to me as soon as I passed that point on my approach to Canada.

She had news indeed: *Will board you at Father Point . . . strictly confidential . . . from Inspector Dew, Scotland Yard, on board* Laurentic.

I replied: *Shall arrive Farther Point about 6 a.m. tomorrow . . . should advise you to come off in small boat with pilot, disguised as pilot . . .*

This was confirmed. The last night was dreary and anxious, the sound of our fog-horn every few minutes adding to the monotony. The hours dragged on as I paced the bridge; now and then I could see Mr Robinson strolling about the deck. I had invited him to get up early to see the 'pilots' come aboard at Father Point in the River St Lawrence. When they did so they came straight to my cabin. I sent for Mr Robinson. When he entered I stood with the detective facing the door, holding my revolver inside my coat pocket. As he came in, I said, 'Let me introduce you.'

Mr Robinson put out his hand, the detective grabbed it, at the same time removing his pilot's cap, and said, 'Good morning, Dr Crippen. Do you know me? I'm Inspector Dew, from Scotland Yard.'

Crippen quivered. Surprise struck him dumb. Then he said, 'Thank God it's over. The suspense has been too great. I couldn't stand it any longer.'

---

promenading walking, strolling
acme the highest degree of something
agog eager and excited
wireless wireless telegraphy, a system of communication using radio waves

Extract from *A Life Inside* by Erwin James

> The following extract is taken from *A Life Inside*, a series
> of columns written for *The Guardian* newspaper by Erwin
> James, a convicted murderer serving a life sentence. Here,
> in a column first published on the 19th February 2004,
> James reflects on the death penalty which was abolished
> in Great Britain in 1965.

A secret graveyard under a prison flowerbed changed the way I serve my time

Buried in the grounds of a small East Midlands prison I was in for much of the 90s are thought to be the remains of some of the prisoners hanged there during the years before the abolition of capital punishment. There is no hard evidence – no gravestones or official notices bearing names or dates. But, during the years I spent there, I heard enough anecdotal evidence to convince me that it was true. The most compelling testimony came from Sister Jean, an elderly woman who had worked as an unpaid assistant to the chaplain for more than 30 years and knew all there was to know about the place.

I had been in the jail just a couple of years when I was

given a job keeping the yards tidy. One February afternoon I was sweeping near the steps of the chapel when Sister Jean stopped to chat. After exchanging pleasantries for a few minutes, I decided to ask her if there was any truth in the rumours. She told me without hesitation.

"They're buried over there where the old outside wall used to be," she said, pointing to a secluded corner six feet or so within the new perimeter wall. "Opposite the topping shed."

The topping shed. There was nothing mythical about the small stone former death house, accessed through a tunnel-shaped annexe a short walk from the main prison wing. Since being decommissioned as a place of execution, the shed had been used as a store for "victuals". When the outside doors were opened for deliveries you could see high up inside. Two robust parallel cross beams stood out from the rest, for no apparent purpose – until you were told. Then it was obvious.

The bulky construction of the beams ensured that they could regularly withstand the sudden jerking weight of a hanged man as he fell through the trap on the platform below. The trap had long since gone, but the platform remained and served admirably as a robust shelf loaded with sacks of oats, flour, and other assorted provisions with which to sustain human life – a typical barb of prison irony.

Once I had learned about the secret burial ground, I

used to take extra care to keep it neat. There was little to see, just a couple of rows of flower beds that had been defeated by the wind, and some shrub borders divided by rarely used earth paths. But it was a beautiful place to spend time thinking and getting my own situation into perspective. However demanding life in prison was, at least I was alive and could still dream about a future.

The funny thing about "the future" when you are serving a life sentence is that you are less sure than most people that it will ever become a reality. You attend review boards where targets are set and checked at the end of a two- or three-year knock-back.

The official perception of your "progress" is set down in reports, and for a while it feels as if you have moved forward. You know the time is passing by the changing of the dates and the seasons, and by the coming and going of fellow prisoners. Then, one day, you take a look around and suddenly it feels like you are still in the exact same place. You thought you were ahead, but all you were doing was treading water, expending all your energy in an effort to stay from going under. But it isn't enough to just survive. You have to survive and then some, if you are ever going to be of any use when the time for release finally arrives.

When Sister Jean told me about the people buried in the prison grounds, I felt more determined than ever. The occasional echo of children's laughter from the other side of the wall when I was over in the corner added to the air of poignancy that seemed to hang about the place. After a stint clearing the litter from the unacknowledged graveyard, a bit of bang-up and the organised chaos on the landings never seemed so bad.

Memories of those prison yards and the secrets they hold have been a motivating factor in the way I have served my time for almost 10 years now. Any moments of disillusionment or times when I could feel myself flagging have been quickly dealt with by a swift recollection of the topping shed conversation with Sister Jean. There is so much about prison that I do not want to remember when the time comes for me to leave. But not the windbeaten flower beds. Those I never want to forget.

Extract from *Set in Darkness* by Ian Rankin

FICTION

> One of the most popular genres of fiction in the 21st century is crime fiction. The following extract is taken from *Set In Darkness*, a novel by the bestselling crime writer Ian Rankin, which was first published in 2000. Here, Inspector Rebus is among a group being given a tour of Queensbury House in Edinburgh, where legend says a kitchen boy was burned to death in the 18th century.

"Hey! Mr Gilfillan! Are you up there?" The voice was coming from below. Gilfillan walked over to a doorway, called down a flight of steps.

"What is it, Marlene?"

"Come take a look."

Gilfillan turned to look at his reluctant group. "Shall we?" He was already heading down. They couldn't very well leave without him. It was stay here, with a bare lightbulb for company, or head down into the basement. Derek Linford led the way.

They came out into a narrow hallway, rooms off to both sides, and other rooms seeming to lead from those. Rebus thought he caught a glimpse of an electrical generator somewhere in the gloom. Voices up ahead and the shadowplay of torches. They walked out of the hallway and into a room lit by a single arc lamp. It was pointing towards a long wall, the bottom half of which had been lined with wooden tongue-and-groove painted the selfsame institutional cream as the plaster walls. Floorboards had been ripped up so that for the most part they were walking on the exposed joists, beneath which sat bare earth. The whole room smelt of damp and mould. Gilfillan and the other archaeologist, the one he'd called Marlene, were crouched in front of this wall, examining the stonework beneath the wood panelling. Two long curves of hewn stone, forming what seemed to Rebus like railway arches in miniature. Gilfillan turned round, looking excited for the first time that day.

"Fireplaces," he said. "Two of them. This must have been the kitchen." He stood up, taking a couple of paces back. "The floor level's been raised at some point. We're only seeing the top half of them." He half-turned towards the group, reluctant to take his eyes off the discovery. "Wonder which one the servant was roasted in . . ."

One of the fireplaces was open, the other closed off by a couple of sections of brown corroding metal.

"What an extraordinary find," Gilfillan said, beaming at his young co-worker. She grinned back at him. It was nice to see people so happy in their work. Digging up the past, uncovering secrets . . . it struck Rebus that they weren't so unlike detectives.

"Any chance of rustling us up a meal then?" Bobby Hogan said, producing a snort of laughter from Ellen Wylie. But Gilfillan wasn't paying any heed. He was standing by the closed fireplace, prying with his fingertips at the space between stonework and metal. The sheet came away easily, Marlene helping him to lift it off and place it carefully on the floor.

"Wonder when they blocked it off?" Grant Hood asked.

Hogan tapped the metal sheet. "Doesn't look exactly prehistoric." Gilfillan and Marlene had lifted away the second sheet. Now everyone was staring at the revealed fireplace. Gilfillan thrust his torch towards it, though the arc lamp gave light enough.

There could be no mistaking the desiccated corpse for anything other than what it was.

Newspaper article on 'youth crime'

The following extract is taken from an article published in *The Independent* newspaper on the 16th May 2014. Here, the writer, Ally Fogg, states who he believes should get the credit for a decline in youth crime.

Who should get credit for declining youth crime? Young people, of course

They are responsible for a record drop in the crime rate, so we should stop demonising them.

Some teenagers tried to rob me the other evening. I was walking my dog on an isolated stretch of the Manchester Cycleway between the run-down neighbourhoods of Gorton and Levenshulme around dusk.

A gang of about half a dozen boys and girls, aged around 15 and sporting urban uniform tracksuit bottoms and hoodies came towards me.

They took one look at my dog, crouched down, and said something approximating: "Oo look atchoo! What a gorgeous liddle puppy wuppy, yesh you are. I'm going to steal you and take you home with me. Come on, come with me doggie . . . "

They then danced off in the opposite direction, with my **pliant** little mutt skipping merrily after them. I let them escape a few yards before calling him to me. As he obediently galloped back, the young bandits gave some melodramatic wails, 'No! Come back!' then we all laughed, waved, and went our separate ways.

This little non-event illustrates a stark but seldom-noted truth about our young people. They are remarkably law-abiding.

The latest statistics from the Ministry of Justice show that the number of people involved with the criminal justice system is at the lowest level since records began in 1970, and the drop is very largely driven by young people.

In 2007 there were 126,500 prosecutions of juveniles, in 2013 there were 48,000. Young people accounted for only 3% of defendants prosecuted in 2013 compared to 7% in 2007.

Over a period of time when the policy of has been to use more and longer custodial sentences, the number of young people in custody has dropped from around 3,000 in 2007/8 to an average of 1,233 last year.

The stubborn remnants of the hell-in-a-handcart brigade will doubtless attribute this to police fiddling their figures, or insist that nobody reports crimes to the police any more.

I hate to splash sunshine on their cherished pessimism, but we see the exact same trends coming through from victim surveys, and from independent sources such as A&E admissions resulting from violent crimes. Some of the crimes which are hardest to sweep under the carpet, such as homicides and firearms offences, have shown some of the largest drops.

The Manchester Cycleway itself offers a vivid example of change. A seven mile stretch of converted railway line, flanked by banks of nettles and far from the reach of police patrols or the **panopticon** gaze of CCTV.

It is the natural habitat of inner city youth, and you do still see them hanging out beneath the countless bridges.

The graffiti in the underpasses has mostly been there for years with nothing added or changed. Twenty, even ten years ago I would not have dared venture there alone and on foot, for fear of the young muggers and gun-toting gangs that once made south Manchester notorious. Today it feels safe, even as night falls.

Of course it is not a utopia. In this city and every other there remain some dangerous individuals and criminal gangs. My dog and I have occasionally had to make a tactical change of route when we sense an air of hostility around the park benches or the underpasses.

Local or national headlines occasionally present us with horrific reminders of humanity's darker side.

There are doubtless some parts of the country where

the improvements to our safety lag far behind the rest. Such exceptions should not leave us blinkered to the rule.

Explanations for the dramatic change in the social landscape of Britain remain hotly debated. There are theories on the table ranging from environmental lead pollution to more effective policing and crime prevention technology, or the acceptability of physical punishment and our growing sensitivity to child abuse.

Others suggest that delinquent criminality has not gone away, but has reinvented itself in less visible incarnations. The truth is most probably a combination of all of the above. However the most obvious and simple solution may be the most significant.

It has long been said that the devil makes work for idle hands, and a lot of juvenile delinquency has always been a product of boredom. It may simply be the case that when young people have a choice of smartphone, tablet and games console in front of them, they feel less need to smash up a bus shelter.

It's true, but having said that, this explanation still seems a trifle **churlish**. As a society we have few hesitations in laying the blame on our young people when things go badly. But we should be equally quick to offer applause when things go right.

The inescapable truth is that young people today are less criminal, less violent, less dangerous than at any time in recent memory, and credit for that goes not to Sony, Apple or Microsoft, but to young people themselves.

pliant easily influenced or controlled
panopticon all-seeing
churlish rude and bad-tempered

The environment

As the 20th and 21st centuries have seen cities grow and urban spaces begin to colonize the countryside, people have increasingly turned to nature to find peace in their busy lives. From rolling meadows to ancient woodland, the beauty and splendour of the natural world have inspired writers from the first decade of the 1900s to the present day.

Environmental issues such as climate change have become increasingly high-profile as humanity's impact on the natural world has been seen. Governments have tried to cut pollution by using renewable forms of energy such as wind and wave power. However, these schemes have sometimes proved controversial, with some arguing that they have a negative impact on the unspoilt beauty of the countryside.

Extract from *The Heart of England* by Edward Thomas

In the early years of the 20th century, the poet and journalist, Edward Thomas, wrote several essays about his journeys in the English countryside, which were later published in *The Heart of England* in 1906. Here, Thomas describes his visit to an old wood.

The chestnut blossom is raining steadily and noiselessly down upon a path whose naked pebbles receive mosaic of emerald light from the interlacing boughs. At intervals, once or twice an hour, the wings of a lonely swallow pass that way, when alone the shower stirs from its **perpendicular** fall. Cool and moist, the perfumed air flows, without lifting the most nervous leaf or letting fall a suspended bead of the night's rain from a honeysuckle bud. In an indefinite sky of grey, through which one **ponderous** cloud billows into sight and is lost again, no sun shines: yet there is light – I know not **whence**; for the brass trappings of the horses beam so as to be extinguished in their own fire. There is no song in wood or sky. Some one of summer's wandering voices – bullfinch or willow-wren – might be singing, but unheard, at least unrealised. From the dead nettle spires, with dull green leaves stained by purple and becoming more and more purple towards the crest, which is of a sombre uniform purple, to the elms reposing at the horizon, all things have bowed the head, hushed, settled into a perfect sleep. Those elms are just visible, no more. The path has no sooner emerged from one shade than another succeeds, and so, on and on, the eye wins no broad **dominion**.

It is a land that uses a soft compulsion upon the passer-by, a compulsion to meditation, which is necessary before he is attached to a scene rather featureless, to a land that **hence** owes much of its power to a mood of generous **reverie** which it **bestows**. And yet it is a land that gives much. Companionable it is, reassuring to the solitary; he soon has a feeling of ease and seclusion there. The cool-leaved wood! The limitless, unoccupied fields of marsh marigold, seen through the trees, most beautiful when the evening rain falls slowly, dimming and almost putting out the **lustrous** bloom! Gold of the minute willows underfoot! Leagues of lonely grass where the slow herds tread the daisies and spare them yet!

Towards night, under the sweet rain, at this warm, skyless close of the day, the trees, far off in an **indolent**, rolling landscape, stand as if disengaged from the world, in a reticent and **pensive repose**.

But suddenly the rain has ceased. In an old, dense wood the last horizontal beams of the sun embrace the trunks of the trees and they glow red under their moist ceiling of green. A stile to be crossed at its edge, where a little stream, unseen, sways the stiff exuberant **angelica** that grows from it, gives the word to pause, and with a rush the silence and the solitude fill the brain. The wood is of uncounted age; the ground on which it stands is more ancient than the surrounding fields, for it rises and falls stormily, with huge boulders here and there; not a path intrudes upon it; the undergrowth is impenetrable to all but fox and bird and this cool red light about the trunks of the trees. Far away a gate is loudly shut, and the rich blue evening comes on and severs me **irrevocably** from all but the light in the old wood and the ghostly white cow-parsley flowers suspended on unseen stalks. And there, among the trees and their shadows, not understood, speaking a forgotten tongue, old dreads and formless awes and fascinations discover themselves and address the comfortable soul, troubling it, recalling to it unremembered years not so long past but that in the end it settles down into a gloomy tranquillity and satisfied discontent, as when we see the place where we were unhappy as children once. Druid and devilish deity and lean wild beast, harmless now, are revolving many memories with me under the strange, sudden red light in the old wood, and not more remote is the league-deep

154

emerald sea-cave from the storm above than I am from the world.

---

perpendicular vertical
ponderous heavy and awkward
whence from where
dominion an area over which someone rules, a domain
hence as a result, therefore
reverie daydreaming
bestow to present with a gift
lustrous bright or brilliant
indolent lazy
pensive deep in thought
repose calm, rest or sleep
angelica a type of herb
irrevocably unable to be altered

Extract from *H is for Hawk* by Helen Macdonald

> The following extract is taken from Helen Macdonald's
> memoir *H is for Hawk*, which was first published in
> 2014. Here, Macdonald describes travelling to an area
> of Cambridgeshire called the Brecklands in search
> of goshawks.

Forty-five minutes north-east of Cambridge is a landscape
I've come to love very much indeed. It's where wet fen
gives way to parched sand. It's a land of twisted pine
trees, burned-out cars, shotgun-peppered road signs and
US Air Force bases. There are ghosts here: houses crumble
inside numbered blocks of pine forestry. There are spaces
built for air-delivered nukes inside grassy **tumuli** behind
twelve-foot fences, tattoo parlours and US Air Force golf
courses. In spring it's a riot of noise: constant plane traffic,
gas-guns over pea fields, wood-larks and jet engines. It's
called the Brecklands – the broken lands – and it's where
I ended up that morning, seven years ago, in early spring,
on a trip I hadn't planned at all. At five in the morning
I'd been staring at a square of streetlight on the ceiling,
listening to a couple of late party-leavers chatting on the

pavement outside. I felt odd: overtired, **overwrought**, unpleasantly like my brain had been removed and my skull stuffed with something like microwaved aluminium foil, dinted, charred and shorting with sparks. *Nnngh. Must get out*, I thought, throwing back the covers. *Out!* I pulled on jeans, boots and a jumper, scalded my mouth with burned coffee, and it was only when my frozen, ancient Volkswagen and I were halfway down the A14 that I worked out where I was going, and why. Out there, beyond the foggy windscreen and white lines, was the forest. The broken forest. That's where I was headed. To see goshawks.

I knew it would be hard. Goshawks *are* hard. Have you ever seen a hawk catch a bird in your back garden? I've not, but I know it's happened. I've found evidence. Out on the patio flagstones, sometimes, tiny fragments: a little, insect-like songbird leg, with a foot clenched tight where the sinews have pulled it; or – even more gruesomely – a **disarticulated** beak, a house-sparrow beak top, or bottom, a little conical bead of blushed gunmetal, slightly translucent, with a few faint **maxillary** feathers adhering to it. But maybe you have: maybe you've glanced out of the window and seen there, on the lawn, a bloody great hawk murdering a pigeon, or a blackbird, or a magpie, and it looks the hugest, most impressive piece of wildness you've ever seen, like someone's tipped a snow leopard into your kitchen and

157

you find it eating the cat. I've had people rush up to me in the supermarket, or in the library, and say, eyes huge, *I saw a hawk catch a bird in my back garden this morning!* And I'm just about to open my mouth and say, *Sparrowhawk!* and they say, 'I looked in the bird book. It was a *goshawk.*' But it never is; the books don't work. When it's fighting a pigeon on your lawn a hawk becomes much larger than life, and bird-book illustrations never match the memory. Here's the sparrowhawk. It's grey, with a black and white barred front, yellow eyes and a long tail. Next to it is the goshawk. This one is also grey, with a black and white barred front, yellow eyes and a long tail. You think, *Hmm.* You read the description. Sparrowhawk: twelve to sixteen inches long. Goshawk: nineteen to twenty-four inches. There. It was huge. It must be a goshawk. They look identical. Goshawks are bigger, that's all. Just bigger.

No. In real life, goshawks resemble sparrowhawks the way leopards resemble housecats. Bigger, yes. But bulkier, bloodier, deadlier, scarier and much, much harder to see. Birds of deep woodland, not gardens, they're the birdwatchers' dark grail. You might spend a week in a forest full of **gosses** and never see one, just traces of their presence. A sudden hush, followed by the calls of terrified woodland birds, and a sense of something moving just beyond vision. Perhaps you'll find a half-eaten pigeon sprawled in a burst of white feathers on the forest floor. Or you might be lucky: walking in a foggy ride at dawn you'll turn your head and catch a split-second glimpse of a bird hurtling past and away, huge taloned feet held loosely clenched, eyes set on a distant target. A split second that stamps the image indelibly on your brain and leaves you hungry for more. Looking for goshawks is like looking for grace: it comes, but not often, and you don't get to say when or how. But you have a slightly better chance on still, clear mornings in early spring, because that's when goshawks **eschew** their world under the trees to court each other in the open sky. That was what I was hoping to see.

I slammed the rusting door, and set off with my binoculars through a forest washed pewter with frost. Pieces of this place had disappeared since I was last here. I found squares of wrecked ground; clear-cut, broken acres with torn roots and drying needles strewn in the sand. Clearings. That's what I needed. Slowly my brain righted itself into spaces unused for months. For so long I'd been living in libraries and college rooms, frowning at screens, marking essays, chasing down academic references. This was a different kind of hunt. Here I was a different animal. Have you ever watched a deer walking out from cover? They step, stop, and stay, motionless, nose to the air, looking and smelling. A nervous twitch might run down their flanks. And then, reassured that all is safe, they ankle their way out of the brush to graze. That morning, I felt like the deer. Not that I was sniffing the air, or standing in fear – but like the deer, I was in the grip of very old and emotional ways of moving through a landscape, experiencing forms of attention and deportment beyond conscious control. Something inside me ordered me how and where to step without me knowing much about it. It might be a million years of evolution, it might be intuition, but on my goshawk hunt I feel tense when I'm walking or standing in sunlight, find myself unconsciously edging towards broken light, or slipping into the narrow, cold shadows along the wide breaks between pine stands. I flinch if I hear a jay calling, or a crow's rolling, angry **alarum**. Both of these things could mean either *Warning, human!* or *Warning, goshawk!* And that morning I was trying to find one by hiding the other. Those old ghostly intuitions that have tied sinew and soul together for millennia had taken over, were doing their thing, making me feel uncomfortable in bright sunlight, uneasy on the wrong side of a ridge, somehow required to walk over the back of a bleached rise of grasses to get to something on the other side: which turned out to be a pond. Small birds rose up in clouds from the pond's edge: chaffinches, bramblings, a flock of long-tailed tits that caught in willow branches like animated cotton buds.

The pond was a bomb crater, one of a line dropped by a German bomber over Lakenheath in the war. It was a watery anomaly, a pond in dunes, surrounded by thick tussocks of sand sedge many, many miles from the sea. I shook my head. It was odd. But then, it's very odd indeed here, and walking the forest you come across all sorts of things you don't expect. Great tracts of reindeer moss, for example: tiny stars and florets and inklings of an ancient flora growing on exhausted land. Crisp underfoot in summer, the stuff is like a patch of the arctic fallen into the world in the wrong place. Everywhere, there are bony shoulders and blades of flint. On wet mornings you can pick up shards knocked from flint cores by Neolithic craftsmen, tiny flakes of stone glowing in thin coats of cold water.

---

tumuli mound of earth and stones
overwrought very upset and nervous or worried
disarticulated separated
maxillary attached to the jaw
gosses goshawks
eschew avoid or abstain from something deliberately
alarum sound of alarm

Newspaper blog about 'wind farms'

A wind farm is a group of wind turbines located in the same area and used to generate electricity. The introduction of wind turbines in the UK has proved controversial, and in the following extract, from a blog first published on *The Telegraph* website on the 16th July 2009, the journalist and writer James Delingpole argues that they blight the countryside.

Wind farms: the death of Britain

"How the hell did we let that happen?" we often ask ourselves when we look at the **brutalist** monstrosity tower blocks which we allowed to blight our towns in the sixties. In a few decades' time we're going to be asking exactly the same question about the 300 foot wind turbines ruining what's left of Britain's wilderness.

And a bit like the perpetrators of terrible sixties architecture now, no one's going to be able to come up with a satisfactory answer because, quite simply, there isn't one: wind turbines are a bad idea in almost every way imaginable.

They don't work when there's no wind.

They don't work when it's too windy.

They produce so little power – and so unreliably and erratically – that even if you put one on every hill top in Britain you'd still need to rely on nuclear, coal and gas-generated electricity for your main source of energy.

They chew up flying wildlife and scare horses.

They produce a subsonic hum which drives you mad if you're downwind of them.

They turn pristine landscape into Teletubby-style horror visions.

They destroy property values.

They steal light.

They're visible for miles around so that just when you're thinking you've got away from it all you're reminded of man's grim presence by the whirling white shapes on the horizon.

They're environmentally damaging: their massive concrete bases alone requiring enough concrete to fill two Olympic-size swimming pools; then there's the access roads that have to be built through the unspoilt landscape to put them up in the first place.

They're twice as expensive as conventionally-produced electricity.

They make you feel a bit queasy, especially the three-bladed ones whose asymmetry is disturbing.

To supply the equivalent output of one nuclear power

station you'd need a wind farm the size of Greater Manchester.

When I wrote all this a couple of years ago in *How To Be Right*, my **polemical** A to Z of everything wrong with Blair's and Brown's Britain, I did think I was erring slightly towards the **Dystopian**.

The "wind turbines" entry was more of a warning of the awful things that *could* go wrong if the more extreme eco-nutters got their way and the government *completely* lost its head. Not even in my darkest moments did I imagine that this nightmare vision would come true.

Why? Well, apart from anything else, because the British landscape is our greatest asset, the thing that makes me so proud to have been born here and to live here. In July, I'll be walking with my family in the near-deserted hills of the Welsh Borders; in late August, I'll be in Scotland wandering amid the purple heather of the Highlands; in October, the coastal path round Prawle Point and Bolt Head. I love swimming in burns, rock pools, rivers, beneath waterfalls, in the sea off South Dorset. I count it one of my greatest privileges to have been hunting over the stone walls of the Cotswolds and the steep valleys of Exmoor. Few things make me happier or more glad to be alive than the joy that so much of our countryside remains so pristine and stunningly beautiful.

And now, in the name of environmentalism, to serve a cause – CO_2 reduction – that will not make the blindest bit of difference to global climate, our Government is destroying this landscape.

brutalist a style of architecture popular in the 1960s, such as concrete
tower blocks
polemical involving an attack in words against someone's opinion or actions
Dystopian relating to a world or society that is frightening and horrible

Extract from *Aurora* by Julie Bertagna

In the 1960s, scientists began to warn about the effects humanity's actions were having on the world's climate. As the 20th century has given way to the 21st, climate change has become an increasingly important issue, inspiring protest and political change. The following extract is taken from the novel *Aurora*, first published in 2011, which depicts a future where rising sea levels have covered most of the world's land and people live either in sky cities or as refugees in boats on the ocean.

Thunder rips through the world, a sound so immense it might be one of the sky towers tumbling down. Pandora unhooks the little brass bugle she keeps on her belt, waits for the thunder to fade, then blows the hardest blast she can muster.

At last, Fox looks down.

'The boats,' he shouts. 'Pan, come and see!'

Pandora pulls dripping locks of hair from amazed green eyes. The great wall that makes an ocean fortress of the sky city, and traps the netherworld in gloom, is the only horizon she has ever known. She has never seen the boat camp beyond, only imagined it clinging like a crop of barnacles to the other side of the wall.

Over the years she and Fox have listened to the crackling voices on the soundwaves: flood refugees telling desperate stories of their survival on the oceans.

They are her people, thinks Pandora, because her lost family must have been boat refugees. Fox chose his netherworld exile; he fled his home in the sky city above to launch the revolution that will soon shake the world. But how did she come to be here? Pandora has no memory of family or a life beyond the wall.

For now, the boat people cling in wretched anchorage around the Earth's sky cities, barricaded under gun shields, crafting weapons from sea junk for the battle ahead. At least, Pandora hopes so. Their communications with the boat camps died in the mighty winter storms. Searching the hissing desolation of the soundwaves, listening for a pulsebeat of the outside world, Pandora has imagined the boat people all swept away.

Step by trembling step, she now begins to climb up the precarious, twisting stairway towards Fox – who takes a sudden leap across empty space and vanishes through an archway.

Pandora searches the darkness. A tiny parapet encircles the top of the spire. Is that where he went? The wind pounds her, fear drums inside, but she climbs on.

'Here.'

His voice is suddenly close. Sheet lightning turns the sky as bright as the moon and Pandora glimpses his ghostly figure in an archway, just above. One last heartstopping twist of the stairway . . . a few more terrifying steps . . .

'Take my hand,' shouts Fox. Rain streams from his outstretched arm. Sweat steams from his skin. If she misjudges the jump, Pandora will follow her lost sword down into the netherworld sea. But she grabs Fox's hand, leaps through the archway – and lands on the narrow parapet at the top of the spire, safe in his grasp. Lightning flickers across their drowned kingdom, illuminating the cathedral that seems to float as an ark in the netherworld sea and the broken bridge that lunges from the water like a lagoon monster, draped in seaweed and barnacled with ancient rust-heaps. All around the old steeple tower and the water-glugged museum, scattered among the massive trunks of the sky towers, lie the last scraps of a city lost to the sea: tiny mudbanked land-scraps, crammed with trees and ruins, teeming with animal life.

Enclosing it all is the vast city wall.

'Look,' urges Fox.

Beyond the wall, as far as she can see, is an immense heaving darkness. The world's ocean!

Science and technology

The scientific progress made in the 20th and 21st centuries has transformed the world. From splitting the atom to the invention of the iPhone, new discoveries and inventions have changed the course of history and created the world we live in today.

Sometimes these scientific achievements have unexpected consequences, such as the discovery of nuclear fission leading to the invention of the atomic bomb. 20th-century authors such as Aldous Huxley have explored the possible darker consequences of cloning and other scientific achievements. However, inventions such as video games have brought pleasure to millions of people and created multi-billion pound industries.

Account of the first radio signal sent across the Atlantic Ocean

On the 12th December 1901 the inventor Guglielmo Marconi successfully received the first radio signal sent across the Atlantic Ocean. Here, he describes awaiting the signal sent from Poldhu in Cornwall in a hut on the cliffs of Newfoundland, a large island off the east coast of Canada.

Shortly before midday I placed the single earphone to my ear and started listening. The receiver on the table before me was very crude – a few coils and condensers and a coherer – no valves, no amplifiers, not even a **crystal**. But I was at last on the point of putting the correctness of all my beliefs to test. The answer came at 12:30 when I heard, faintly but distinctly, *pip-pip-pip*. I handed the phone to Kemp: "Can you hear anything?" I asked. "Yes," he said. "The letter S." He could hear it. I knew then that all my anticipations had been justified. The electric waves sent out into space from Poldhu had traversed the Atlantic – the distance, enormous as it seemed then, of 1,700 miles – unimpeded by the curvature of the earth. The result meant much more to me than the mere successful realization of an experiment. As Sir Oliver Lodge has stated, it was an **epoch** in history. I now felt for the first time absolutely certain that the day would come when mankind would be able to send messages without wires not only across the Atlantic but between the farthermost ends of the earth.

crystal crystal detector, used to power a radio receiver
epoch a period of time marked by particular events

Extract from *'Atom-Splitting'*, a newspaper article by J. B. S. Haldane

> In 1938 scientists discovered nuclear fission, an achievement that revolutionized science and led to the invention of the atomic bomb. In this newspaper article, which was first published in March 1939, the scientist J. B. S. Haldane explains the implications of this discovery.

This is a sensational article. I am sorry. In these articles I try to keep to the facts. But occasionally facts are sensational. A discovery has just been made which may revolutionize human life as completely as the steam engine, and much more quickly. The odds are against its doing so, but not more than ten to one, if so much. So it is worth writing about it.

In the *Daily Worker* of March 30th, 1939, I described the recent work on splitting the nuclei of uranium atoms. A certain number of them explode when neutrons collide with them. Neutrons are among the so-called elementary particles – that is to say, particles which have not yet been broken up, such as electrons, protons, and perhaps a few others. This does not mean that they will never be broken up.

Ordinary atoms hold together when they collide at a speed of about a mile a second, as they do in air. When the temperature is raised and the speed of collisions goes up to ten miles or so a second, they cannot hold together, but electrons – that is to say, elementary particles with a negative charge – are torn off them. That is why a flame conducts electricity.

But at moderate speeds – say, a few thousand miles per second – collisions only break up the atoms temporarily. They soon pick up their lost electrons. When the speed rises to tens or hundreds of thousands of miles per second, the nuclei, or cores of the atoms, are sometimes broken up.

When a current is passed through the heavy variety of hydrogen at a voltage of half a million or so, the atomic nuclei become formidable projectiles, and if they hit a light metal called lithium they break up its atomic nuclei and let neutrons loose. Neutrons can penetrate the nuclei of many atoms even when moving slowly and cause still further changes.

Generally they only chip a piece off. But when they attack uranium, an element which is unstable anyway, and produces radium, though very slowly, when left to itself, the uranium nuclei split up. The new fact, first discovered by **Joliot** and his colleagues in Paris, is that when the uranium nucleus splits, it produces neutrons also. In the experiments so far made, very small pieces of uranium were used.

So most of the neutrons, which can penetrate even metals for some distance, get out. But if the neutrons are **liberated** in the middle of a sufficiently large lump of uranium, they will cause further nuclei to break up, and the process will spread. The principle involved is quite simple. A single stick burns with difficulty, because most of the heat gets away. But a large pile of sticks will blaze, even if most of them are damp.

Nobody knows how large a lump of uranium is needed before it begins to set itself alight, so to say. But experiments are already under way in two British and one German laboratory to my knowledge, and doubtless in others in America, the Soviet Union and elsewhere.

In the current number [May 13th, 1939] of *Nature* Joliot and **Halban**, a French and a German physicist working together in Paris, published an S.O.S. letter suggesting means for slowing the process down, so as to avoid disaster.

If the experiment succeeds several things may happen. The change may take place slowly, the metal gradually warming up. It may occur fairly quickly, in which case there will be a mild explosion, and the lump will fly apart into vapour before one atom in a million has been affected. Or there may be a really big explosion. For if about one four-hundredth of the mass of the exploding uranium is converted into energy, as seems to be probable, an ounce would produce enough heat to boil about 1,000 tons of water. So 1 oz. of uranium, if it exploded suddenly, would be equivalent to over 100,000 tons of high explosive.

Joliot Frédéric Joliot-Curie, a French physicist
liberated freed
Halban Hans von Halban, a German physicist

Extract from *Surely You're Joking, Mr Feynman* by Richard Feynman

Following the outbreak of the Second World War, the US government recruited a team of scientists to develop the atomic bomb. Richard Feynman was one of these scientists and in the following extract taken from his memoir *Surely You're Joking, Mr Feynman*, which was first published in 1985, he describes witnessing the test explosion of the first atomic bomb in 1945.

I flew back, and I arrived just when the buses were leaving, so I went straight out to the site and we waited out there, twenty miles away. We had a radio, and they were supposed to tell us when the thing was going to go off and so forth, but the radio wouldn't work, so we never knew what was happening. But just a few minutes before it was supposed to go off the radio started to work, and they told us there was twenty seconds or something to go, for people who were far away like we were. Others were closer, six miles away.

They gave out dark glasses that you could watch it with. Dark glasses! Twenty miles away, you couldn't see a damn thing through dark glasses. So I figured the only thing that could really hurt your eyes (bright light can never hurt your eyes) is ultraviolet light. I got behind a truck windshield, because the ultraviolet can't go through glass, so that would be safe, and so I could see the damn thing.

Time comes, and this tremendous flash out there is so bright that I duck, and I see this purple splotch on the floor of the truck. I said, "That's not it. That's an after-image." So I look back up, and I see this white light changing into yellow and then into orange. Clouds form and disappear again – from the compression and expansion of the shock wave.

Finally, a big ball of orange, the center that was so bright, becomes a ball of orange that starts to rise and billow a little bit and get a little black around the edges, and then you see it's a big ball of smoke with flashes on the inside, with the heat of the fire going outwards.

All this took about one minute. It was a series from bright to dark, and I had seen it. I am about the only guy who actually looked at the damn thing – the first Trinity test. Everybody else had dark glasses, and the people at six miles couldn't see it because they were all told to lie on the floor. I'm probably the only guy who saw it with the human eye.

Finally, after about a minute and a half, there's suddenly a tremendous noise—BANG, and then a rumble, like thunder – and that's what convinced me. Nobody had said a word during this whole thing. We were all just watching quietly. But this sound released everybody – released me particularly because the solidity of the sound at that distance meant that it had really worked.

The man standing next to me said, "What's that?"

I said, "That was the Bomb."

The man was William Laurence. He was there to write an article describing the whole situation. I had been the one who was supposed to have taken him around. Then it was found that it was too technical for him, and so later H. D. Smyth came and I showed him around. One thing we did, we went into a room and there on the end of a narrow pedestal was a small silver-plated ball. You could put your hand on it. It was warm. It was radioactive. It was plutonium. And we stood at the door of this room, talking about it. This was a new element that was made by man, that had never existed on the earth before, except for a very short period possibly at the very beginning. And here it was all isolated and radioactive and had these properties. And we had made it. And so it was tremendously valuable.

Meanwhile, you know how people do when they talk – you kind of jiggle around and so forth. He was kicking the doorstop, you see, and I said, "Yes, the doorstop certainly is appropriate for this door." The doorstop was a ten-inch hemisphere of yellowish metal – gold, as a matter of fact.

What had happened was that we needed to do an experiment to see how many neutrons were reflected by different materials, in order to save the neutrons so we didn't use so much material. We had tested many different materials. We had tested platinum, we had tested zinc, we had tested brass, we had tested gold. So, in making the tests with the gold, we had these pieces of gold and somebody had the clever idea of using that great ball of gold for a doorstop for the door of the room that contained the plutonium.

After the thing went off, there was tremendous excitement at Los Alamos. Everybody had parties, we all ran around. I sat on the end of a jeep and beat drums and so on. But one man, I remember, Bob Wilson, was just sitting there moping.

I said, "What are you moping about?"

He said, "It's a terrible thing that we made."

I said, "But you started it. You got us into it."

You see, what happened to me – what happened to the rest of us – is we started for a good reason, then you're working very hard to accomplish something and it's a pleasure, it's excitement. And you stop thinking, you know; you just stop. Bob Wilson was the only one who was still thinking about it, at that moment.

Extract from *Brave New World* by Aldous Huxley

Scientific discoveries can have a huge impact on society. In his 1932 novel *Brave New World*, Aldous Huxley imagines a world where a scientific procedure called the Bokanovsky Process is used to produce human clones, with society divided into five classes. Here, he describes how babies from the lower class known as Delta are experimented on in order to condition them not to read books or appreciate flowers.

The nurses stiffened to attention as the D.H.C. came in.

"Set out the books," he said curtly.

In silence the nurses obeyed his command. Between the rose bowls the books were duly set out – a row of nursery quartos opened invitingly each at some gaily coloured image of beast or fish or bird.

"Now bring in the children."

They hurried out of the room and returned in a minute or two, each pushing a kind of tall dumb-waiter laden, on all its four wire-netted shelves, with eight-month-old babies, all exactly alike (a Bokanovsky Group, it was evident) and all (since their **caste** was Delta) dressed in khaki.

"Put them down on the floor."

The infants were unloaded.

"Now turn them so that they can see the flowers and books."

Turned, the babies at once fell silent, then began to crawl towards those clusters of sleek colours, those shapes so gay and brilliant on the white pages. As they approached, the sun came out of a momentary eclipse behind a cloud. The roses flamed up as though with a sudden passion from within; a new and profound significance seemed to suffuse the shining pages of the books. From the ranks of the crawling babies came little squeals of excitement, gurgles and twitterings of pleasure.

The Director rubbed his hands. "Excellent!" he said. "It might almost have been done on purpose."

The swiftest crawlers were already at their goal. Small hands reached out uncertainly, touched, grasped, unpetaling the transfigured roses, crumpling the illuminated pages of the books. The Director waited until all were happily busy. Then, "Watch carefully," he said. And, lifting his hand, he gave the signal.

The Head Nurse, who was standing by a switchboard at the other end of the room, pressed down a little lever.

There was a violent explosion. Shriller and ever shriller, a siren shrieked. Alarm bells maddeningly sounded.

The children started, screamed; their faces were distorted with terror.

"And now," the Director shouted (for the noise was deafening), "now we proceed to rub in the lesson with a mild electric shock."

He waved his hand again, and the Head Nurse pressed a second lever.

The screaming of the babies suddenly changed its tone. There was something desperate, almost insane, about the sharp spasmodic yelps to which they now gave utterance. Their little bodies twitched and stiffened; their limbs moved jerkily as if to the tug of unseen wires.

"We can electrify that whole strip of floor," bawled the Director in explanation. "But that's enough," he signalled to the nurse.

The explosions ceased, the bells stopped ringing, the shriek of the siren died down from tone to tone into silence. The stiffly twitching bodies relaxed, and what had become the sob and yelp of infant maniacs broadened out once more into a normal howl of ordinary terror.

"Offer them the flowers and the books again."

The nurses obeyed; but at the approach of the roses, at the mere sight of those gaily-coloured images of pussy and cock-a-doodle-doo and baa-baa black sheep, the infants shrank away in horror, the volume of their howling suddenly increased.

"Observe," said the Director triumphantly, "observe."

Books and loud noises, flowers and electric shocks-already in the infant mind these couples were compromisingly linked; and after two hundred repetitions of the same or a similar lesson would be **wedded indissolubly**. What man has joined, nature is powerless to put asunder.

"They'll grow up with what the psychologists used to call an 'instinctive' hatred of books and flowers. Reflexes unalterably conditioned. They'll be safe from books and botany all their lives." The Director turned to his nurses. "Take them away again."

Still yelling, the khaki babies were loaded on to their dumb-waiters and wheeled out, leaving behind them the smell of sour milk and a most welcome silence.

---

caste class
wedded joined together
indissolubly with no possibility of being undone

Extract from *Trigger Happy* by Steven Poole

The following extract is taken from *Trigger Happy*, a non-fiction book exploring the history and appeal of videogames which was first published in 2000. Here, the writer explains the history of his own love of videogames.

Like millions of people, I love videogames. I also love books, music and chess. That's not unusual. For most of my generation, videogames are just part of the cultural furniture. In particular, videogames, among people all over the world, are a social pleasure. The after-hours PlayStation session is one of the joys of modern life.

Videogames are in one sense just another entertainment choice – but compared to many, a much more interesting one. And yet there seems to be a fear that videogames are somehow nudging out other art forms, and that we're encouraging a generation of screen-glazed androids with no social skills, poetical sensitivity or entrepreneurial ambition. But new forms don't replace the old. Film did not replace theatre. The Internet did not replace the book. Videogames have been around for thirty years, and they're not going away.

When I was ten years old, my parents bought me a home computer. It was a ZX Spectrum, brainchild of the celebrated British inventor Sir Clive Sinclair (this was before he went on to create the savagely unsuccessful electric tricycle called the C5). The entire computer, which was a contemporary of the American Commodore Vic-20, was about half the size of a modern PC keyboard, and it plugged into a normal television. It was black, with little gray squidgy keys and a rainbow stripe over one corner. Tiny blocky characters would move around blocky landscapes lavishly painted in eight colors, while the black box beeped and burped. It was pure witchcraft. But the magic wasn't simply done to me; it was a spell I could dive into. I could swim happily in this world, at once mysterious and utterly logical, of insubstantial light.

Doubtless my parents imagined the Spectrum would be educational. In a way it was, for very soon I was an expert at setting exactly the right recording levels on hi-fi equipment to ensure a perfect copy of a hot new game. (In those days, videogames came on cassette, and I would swap copies and hints with my schoolfriends.) For many years, the myriad delights that videogames offered were a reliable evening escape, their names now a peculiarly evocative roll call of sepia-tinged pleasures: Jet Pac, Ant Attack, Manic Miner, Knight Lore, Way of the Exploding Fist, Dark Star . . . Then I decided, at the age of sixteen, to put away childish things. So I bought a guitar and formed a skate-punk heavy-metal band.

Extract from *iPod, Therefore I Am: A Personal Journey Through Music* by Dylan Jones

> In the following extract from his book published in 2005, the writer Dylan Jones explains his obsession with the iPod.

'How the iPod changed my life'

I've always loved my toys. As a kid it was Lego, Meccano, Subbuteo and Scalextric.

Then, when I was a teenager, it was my racing bike, my stereo and skateboard. Eventually, I became obsessed with cars, too.

But the last time I became besotted with a piece of hardware was in the 80s, when I bought my first Sony Walkman.

This was the life, I thought, a machine that plays the latest Adam & The Ants album as I sat on the bus to college. What could be cooler than that?

Well, the iPod, actually. Which is probably the coolest thing in the world right now. A boy's toy that's also a girl's toy. A toy I've become utterly obsessed with.

It happened about 18 months ago. My wife asked me what I wanted for Christmas and, as I always want the latest toy, I suggested an iPod.

"You're mad," said a friend who works in the music business (ironically). "How much time do you have to yourself? When will you ever use it?"

But the fear of being left behind by the iPod generation was stronger than the fear that I might never use the thing . . .

And my world turned upside down. Here was a machine that didn't just play the new Adam & The Ants LP, if I wanted it to (which I didn't). It would play every Adam & The Ants song ever recorded.

This little white plastic box could store up to 10,000 of my favourite songs. And while I realised that there probably weren't 10,000 songs I actually liked, I was sure I could fill it with at least 5,000.

And so I started filleting my record collection and uploading them on to iTunes. I began spending every available minute rummaging through every CD, album, single and cassette, looking for songs worthy of my new baby. On day two, I discovered I had Hunky Dory not just on CD but on cassette and also twice on vinyl. The album was one of David Bowie's most formative but did I need five copies?

The process of deciding what to upload was tantamount to listening to every song I'd ever bought.

Some were imported immediately but many more were forced to walk my PowerBook's metaphorical plank. Would I rip it into an MP3 or press eject?

Over the next six months, I began loading my iPod as though my life depended on it. Not only did I go through every single CD and upload the songs I liked, I also recorded all of my vinyl and then began downloading songs from the internet (legally, of course).

In the space of just a few months I was totally addicted.

I fell in love with the process immediately. As soon as the song was uploaded, the file just lay there, nameless, blameless.

And so I would type in the artist's name, the song title, the album it came from (as well as host of other categories) and then watch it flip into its rightful alphabetical place.

And having spent a few nights doing this, my friend Robin, who had already become well versed in the ways of the Pod, said I should upload while connected to the internet, as the program would then download the information for you.

Fantastic! My own private radio station was being compiled right before my eyes – all I had to do was upload the content.

As soon as I got busy with my new toy, experts popped up everywhere . . . Was I going to start burning CDs, 70 minutes of personalised taste to give to friends and family? Was I going to move up a gear and burn my first MP3 CD, a full eight-and-a-half hours of compressed digital fun? How was I doing with smart playlists? Was I making my own CD covers yet? Had I downloaded anything from Limewire?

This was all before me, as what I was really enjoying was editing my life. I had spent far too much time compiling cassettes of my favourite music – 120-minute juxtapositions of the cool and the corny. Esoteric Springsteen or doo-wop compilations, the A-Z of the Beatles, the A-B of Will Young.

In my late-20s, I began a series of One Louder cassettes, in homage to Spinal Tap, reaching 21 Louder before running out of steam.

But there were plenty of others, too – Terminal 1970s Freeway Madness (Side 1: Fast Lane, Side 2: Slow Lane, you get the picture), Disco Epiphany, Disco Nirvana, Now That's What I Call REM, 100 Minutes Of The Clash, The Best Beach Boys Tape In The World, Everything She Wants (a shed-load of Wham! for an ex-girlfriend) . . .

Albums ceased to matter. Why bother with REM's New Adventures In Hi-Fi when all you really want is Electrolite and E-Bow The Letter? Why continue to ruin Pet Sounds by suffering the absurdity of Sloop John B when you can simply delete it?

Having embraced iTunes, I could now listen to the Beatles albums without the Ringo tracks. My version of The Clash's Give 'Em Enough Rope no longer included

Julie's Been Working For The Drug Squad, while Stairway To Heaven had miraculously vanished from my edition of Led Zeppelin IV.

The iPod not only changed the way I felt about music, it helped me re-establish relationships with records I hadn't heard in years.

Bad Company's I Can't Get Enough Of Your Love became a constant companion, as did Ace's How Long and Cracker's Low.

Zero 7 became gods, as did the Yellow Magic Orchestra, Eno, Phoenix, Bob Seger and The Bees.

Every record I've ever owned and kept is now on my machine, from David Bowie's Starman right up to Shapeshifter's happy house classic Lola's Theme.

One is a record I bought after seeing it performed on Top Of The Pops, the other after I heard it in an Ibizan nightclub.

My whole life is here, 40Gb of memory, 30 years of memories. Every song I've ever cared about is in here somewhere, waiting in its chosen spot, hugging the wall until it's chosen to dance.

Not only has the iPod changed the way I listen to music, it has changed my life, too.

Like my old Walkman, I am never without it. I listen to it as I walk to work, as I lie in bed, as I eat my lunch. I'm listening to it right now, as I write this.

And you know what? It sounds good.

Exploration and adventure

In the early years of the 20th century, explorers finally conquered some of the remotest places on Earth. In 1912, Roald Amundsen led the first expedition to reach the South Pole, narrowly beating the British team led by Sir Robert Falcon Scott, who perished on their return from the Pole. After many unsuccessful attempts, the summit of Mount Everest, the highest mountain in the world, was finally reached by Edmund Hillary and Tenzing Norgay in 1953.

In the later years of the 20th century and into the 21st, such exploits have increasingly been undertaken by adventure tourists, with the availability of package holidays to Antarctica and Mount Everest. The very richest tourists have even made their way into orbit, as space exploration has moved from science fiction to fact, with humanity reaching the Moon and now looking to Mars and beyond.

Extract from *The Missing of the Somme* by Geoff Dyer

LITERARY NON-FICTION

> The following extract is taken from Geoff Dyer's book-length essay *The Missing of the Somme*, which was first published in 2011. Here he describes and contrasts the British and Norwegian expeditions which set out in 1911 to conquer the South Pole.

Between November 1911 and January 1912 two teams of men – one British, headed by a naval officer, Robert Falcon Scott, the other Norwegian, headed by Roald Amundsen – were engaged in the last stage of a protracted race to the South Pole. Using dogs and adapting themselves skilfully to the hostile environment, the Norwegian team reached the Pole on 15 December and returned safely. Scott, leader of an ill-prepared expedition which relied on strength-sapping man-hauling, reached the Pole on 17 January. Defeated, the five-man team faced a gruelling 800-mile trudge back to safety. By 21 March, eleven miles from the nearest depot of food and fuel, the three exhausted surviving members of the expedition – Scott, Dr Edward Wilson and Henry Bowers – pitched their tent and sat out a blizzard. At some point Scott seems to have made the decision that it was better to stay put and preserve the record of their struggle rather than die in their tracks. They survived for at least nine days while Scott, in Roland Huntford's phrase, 'prepared his exit from the stage' and addressed letters to posterity: 'We are setting a good example to our countrymen, if not by getting into a tight place, by facing it like men when we get there.' Despite its failure, the expedition, wrote Scott, 'has shown that Englishmen can endure hardships, help one another and meet death with as great a **fortitude** as ever in the past'. The tradition of heroic death which **aggrandizes** his own example is also invigorated by it: 'We are showing that Englishmen can still die with a bold spirit, fighting it out to the end . . .. I think this makes an example for Englishmen of the future.'

On 12 November, in the collapsed tent, the bodies and their documents were found by a rescue party and the legend of Scott of the Antarctic began to take immediate effect. 'Of their suffering, hardship and devotion to one another,' wrote a member of the rescue team, 'the world will soon know the deeds that were done were equally as great as any committed on Battlefield and won the respect and honour of every true Britisher.'

Scott's headstrong incompetence had actually meant that, from an early stage, the expedition had been riddled by tension. Captain Oates – the 'very gallant Englishman' of legend – had earlier written that 'if Scott fails to get to the Pole he jolly well deserves it'. Although clad in the guise of scientific discovery, Scott's expedition contributed nothing to the knowledge of polar travel unless it was to emphasize 'the grotesque **futility** of man-hauling'. But with Scott, futility (the title of one of only a handful of poems published by Wilfred Owen in his lifetime) becomes an important component of the heroic. That Scott had turned the expedition into an affair of 'heroism for heroism's sake' only enhanced the **posthumous** glory that greeted news of his death when it reached England on 11 February the following year.

A memorial service 'for one of the most inefficient of polar expeditions, and one of the worst of polar explorers' was held at St Paul's, and Scott's failure took its place alongside Nelson's victory at Trafalgar as a triumphant expression of the British spirit. Scott's distorting, highly **rhetorical** version of events was taken up enthusiastically and unquestioningly by the nation as a whole. At the naval dockyard chapel in Devonport, the sermon emphasized 'the glory of self-sacrifice, the blessing of failure'. By now the glorious failure personified by Scott had become a British ideal: a vivid example of how 'to make a virtue of **calamity** and dress up incompetence as heroism'.

fortitude strength
aggrandizes enhances the reputation of someone beyond what is justified by the facts
futility uselessness
posthumous happening after a person's death
rhetorical (referring to language) used for impressive effect
calamity an event that causes great damage or distress

Extract from the diary of Captain Robert Falcon Scott

> The following extract is taken from Sir Robert Falcon Scott's diary and was written on either the 16th or 17th March 1912. This entry describes the last days of the Antarctic explorer's failed expedition to be the first to reach the South Pole.

Friday, March 16 or Saturday 17 – Lost track of dates, but think the last correct. Tragedy all along the line. At lunch, the day before yesterday, poor Titus Oates said he couldn't go on; he proposed we should leave him in his sleeping-bag. That we could not do, and we induced him to come on, on the afternoon march. In spite of its awful nature for him he struggled on and we made a few miles. At night he was worse and we knew the end had come.

Should this be found I want these facts recorded. Oates' last thoughts were of his Mother, but immediately before he took pride in thinking that his regiment would be pleased with the bold way in which he met his death. We can testify to his bravery. He has **borne** intense suffering for weeks without complaint, and to the very last was able and willing to discuss outside subjects. He did not – would not – give up hope till the very end. He was a brave soul. This was the end. He slept through the night before last, hoping not to wake; but he woke in the morning – yesterday. It was blowing a blizzard. He said, 'I am just going outside and may be some time.' He went out into the blizzard and we have not seen him since.

---

borne endured

Account of George Leigh Mallory's attempt to climb Mount Everest

The first British expedition to climb Mount Everest set out in 1922, led by Charles G. Bruce and accompanied by a team of mountaineers including George Mallory. Here, Mallory describes how an avalanche ended his attempt to reach the mountain's peak. This account was first published in *The Assault on Mount Everest* by Charles G. Bruce in 1923.

The scene was peculiarly bright and windless, and as we rarely spoke, nothing was to be heard but the laboured panting of our lungs. This stillness was suddenly disturbed. We were startled by an ominous sound, sharp, arresting, violent, and yet somehow soft like an explosion of **untamped** gunpowder. I had never before on a mountainside heard such a sound; but all of us, I imagine, knew instinctively what it meant, as though we had been accustomed to hear it every day of our lives. In a moment I observed the surface of the snow broken and puckered where it had been even for a few yards to the right of me. I took two steps convulsively in this direction with some quick thought of getting nearer to the edge of the danger that threatened us. And then I began to move slowly downwards, inevitably carried on the whole moving surface by a force I was utterly powerless to resist. Somehow I managed to turn out from the slope so as to avoid being pushed headlong and backwards down it. For a second or two I seemed hardly to be in danger as I went quietly sliding down with the snow. Then the rope at my waist tightened and held me back. A wave of snow came over me and I was buried. I supposed that the matter was settled. However, I called to mind experiences related by other parties; and it had been suggested that the best chance of escape in this situation lay in swimming. I thrust out my arms above my head and actually went through some sort of motions of swimming on my back. Beneath the surface of the snow, with nothing to inform the senses of the world outside it, I had no impression of speed after the first acceleration – I struggled in the tumbling snow, unconscious of everything else – until, perhaps only a few seconds later, I knew the pace was easing up. I felt an increasing pressure about my body. I wondered how tightly I should be squeezed, and then the avalanche came to rest.

My arms were free; my legs were near the surface. After a brief struggle, I was standing again, surprised and breathless, in the motionless snow. But the rope was tight at my waist; the porter tied on next me, I supposed, must be deeply buried. To my further surprise, he quickly emerged, unharmed as myself. Somervell and Crawford too, though they had been above me by the rope's length, were now quite close, and soon extricated themselves. We subsequently made out that their experiences had been very similar to mine. But where were the rest? Looking down over the foam of snow, we saw one group of porters some little distance, perhaps 150 ft, below us. Presumably the others must be buried somewhere between us and them, and though no sign of these missing men appeared, we at once prepared to find and dig them out. The porters we saw still stood their ground instead of coming up to help. We soon made out that they were the party who had been immediately behind us, and they were pointing below them. They had travelled farther than us in the avalanche, presumably because they were nearer the centre, where it was moving more rapidly. The other two parties, one of four and one of five men roped together, must have been carried even farther. We could still hope that they were safe. But as we hurried down we soon saw that beneath the place where the four porters were standing was a formidable drop; it was only too plain that the missing men had been swept over it. We had no difficulty in finding a way round this obstacle; in a very short time we were standing under its shadow. The ice-cliff was from forty to sixty feet high in different places; the crevasse at its foot was more or less filled up with avalanche snow. Our fears were soon confirmed. One man was quickly uncovered and found to be still breathing; before long we were certain that he would live. Another whom we dug out near him had been killed by the fall. He and his party appeared to have struck the hard lower lip of the crevasse, and were lying under the snow on or near the edge of it. The four porters who had escaped soon pulled themselves together after the first shock of the accident, and now worked here with Crawford and did everything they could to extricate the other bodies, while Somervell and I went down into the crevasse. A loop of rope which we pulled up convinced us that the other party must be here. It was slow work loosening the snow with the pick or adze of an ice-axe and shovelling it with the hands. But we were able to fallow the rope to the bodies. One was dug up lifeless; another was found upside down, and when we uncovered his face Somervell thought he was still breathing.

We had the greatest difficulty in extricating this man, so tightly was the snow packed about his limbs; his load, four oxygen cylinders on a steel frame, had to be cut from his back, and eventually he was dragged out. Though buried for about forty minutes, he had survived the fall and the suffocation, and suffered no serious harm. Of the two others in this party of four, we found only one. We had at length to give up a hopeless search with the certain knowledge that the first of them to be swept over the cliff, and the most deeply buried, must long ago be dead. Of the other five, all the bodies were recovered, but only one was alive. The two who had so marvellously escaped were able to walk down to Camp III, and were almost perfectly well next day. The other seven were killed.

---

untamped without a fuse

Newspaper article about adventure tourism

> In 2012 a photograph was published showing a long line of climbers queuing to ascend Mount Everest. In this newspaper article, which was first published on the 30th May 2012, Jonathan Jones criticizes this kind of adventure tourism.

Behold Mount Everest, reduced to adventure tourism

This is a photograph of all that has gone wrong in humanity's relationship with nature. Amid the rocky vastness of Mount Everest, a long line of people stand in the snow in a bizarre pedestrian traffic jam. Four people recently died on a single day on Everest: on that day 150 climbers made the ascent. It has been claimed that human traffic jams contributed to the tragedy, which seems only too likely looking at this picture. But as well as helping to explain those deaths, it is a picture of how profoundly we are failing to have any kind of decent respect for our world: how our romance with nature has become sick and twisted.

Britons are currently looking back at 60 years of history. The popularity of the Queen's diamond jubilee surely has less to do with reverence for majesty than a recognition that Elizabeth II's reign spans 60 years of history: thinking ourselves back to its start, we get a perspective on a period of radical change. As it happens, one of the most memorable events at the start of the Queen's reign was the "conquest" of Everest by a Commonwealth expedition. On 29 May 1953 Tenzing Norgay and Edmund Hillary became the first human beings who are ever known to have stood on the summit of the world's highest mountain.

It is instructive to compare today's photograph of an ant-like line of climbers with Hillary's picture of Tenzing Norgay on top of Everest. In the 1953 photograph one man stands alone on the snow-clad summit, seeming almost on the edge of space itself as a deep, dark blue void surrounds his thickly clad form. This image of the solitary explorer of lofty mountain realms has its chilly feet in early 19th century Romanticism: Tenzing Norgay is alone on the mountain, just like Caspar David Friedrich's Wanderer above the Sea of Mist in the 1818 painting that perfectly expresses the Romantic affinity for remote heights.

Mountain climbing as a sport grew out of the Romantic movement. Sir Walter Scott's poem Helvellyn tells of his own solitary ascent of the Lakelands peak and meditates on the death of a hiker there, whose body was guarded by his sole companion, a faithful dog: such images of distance from the everyday crowded world – and of lonely death – are integral to the myth of mountaineering still very much alive in tales such as **Touching the Void**.

This photograph mocks that romance. It shows an Everest that has merely become an overcrowded destination for extreme tourists who can afford to pay from 10 to fifty thousand dollars for something different and exotic. An ascent of Mount Everest is no longer the achievement at the edge of possibility that it was back in 1953 on the eve of the space age. If we want to know why so many people are preparing to nostalgically relive the early 1950s this weekend we might contemplate this high altitude tailback and reflect that a great deal of innocence has gone from the world. The picture of Everest's numerous ascendants reveals not only the excess of commercialised adventure tourism but the mind-warping impact of technology: why on earth do we believe there should be "progress" in ascending Everest? That this of all things should become easier and more accessible?

We believe it because we believe everything is becoming easier, faster, and more democratic. Technological advances, better clothes, better oxygen supplies, make what once took years of planning and a nationally sponsored expedition possible for anyone with the cash – we assume. Nature, from being a terror, has become a tame toy in the modern imagination.

Which is, of course, an illusion. Everest is not tame. The idea that it is controllable has been exposed once again as a spurious fantasy. Modern communications do not save you when you are too high for helicopters. The crowds queue past the dead and dying. This sad surreal image is not just about Everest but captures the delusions that hasten the world towards environmental catastrophe.

Touching the Void a memoir by the mountaineer Joe Simpson

Extract from *The Cruelest Journey* by Kira Salak

> The following extract is taken from *The Cruelest Journey*, which was first published in 2004. Here the writer and adventurer Kira Salak describes the beginning of her 600-mile journey travelling solo in a kayak from Old Ségou in Mali to Timbuktu, following the route taken by the 19th century explorer, Mungo Park.

In the beginning, my journeys feel at best ludicrous, at worst insane. This one is no exception. The idea is to paddle nearly 600 miles on the Niger River in a kayak, alone, from the Malian town of Old Ségou to Timbuktu. And now, at the very hour when I have decided to leave, a thunderstorm bursts open the skies, sending down apocalyptic rain, washing away the very ground beneath my feet. It is the rainy season in Mali, for which there can be no comparison in the world. Lightning pierces trees, slices across houses. Thunder racks the skies and pounds the earth like mortar fire, and every living thing huddles in tenuous shelter, expecting the world to end. Which it doesn't. At least not this time. So that we all give a collective sigh to the salvation of the passing storm as it rumbles its way east, and I survey the river

I'm to leave on this morning. Rain or no rain, today is the day for the journey to begin. And no one, not even the oldest in the village, can say for certain whether I'll get to the end.

"Let's do it," I say, leaving the shelter of an **adobe** hut. My guide from town, Modibo, points to the north, to further storms. He says he will pray for me. It's the best he can do. To his knowledge, no man has ever completed such a trip, though a few have tried. And certainly no woman has done such a thing. This morning he took me aside and told me he thinks I'm crazy, which I understood as concern and thanked him. He told me that the people of Old Ségou think I'm crazy too, and that only uncanny good luck will keep me safe.

What he doesn't know is that the worst thing a person can do is tell me that I can't do something, because then I'll want to do it all the more. It may be a failing of mine. I carry my inflatable kayak through the narrow passageways of Old Ségou, past the small adobe huts melting in the rains, past the huddling goats and smoke of cooking fires, people peering out at me from the dark entranceways. It is a labyrinth of ancient homes, built and rebuilt after each storm, plastered with the very earth people walk upon. Old Ségou must look much the same as it did in Scottish explorer Mungo Park's time when, exactly 206 years ago to the day, he left on the first of his two river journeys down the Niger to Timbuktu, the first such trip by a Westerner. It is no coincidence that I've planned to leave on the same day and from the same spot. Park is my benefactor of sorts, my guarantee. If he could travel down the Niger, then so can I. And it is all the guarantee I have for this trip – that an obsessed nineteenth-century adventurer did what I would like to do. Of course Park also died on this river, but I've so far managed to overlook that.

Hobbled donkeys cower under a new onslaught of rain, ears back, necks craned. Little naked children dare each other to touch me, and I make it easy for them, stopping and holding out my arm. They stroke my white skin as if it were velvet, using only the pads of their fingers, then stare at their hands for wet paint.

Thunder again. More rain falls. I stop on the shore, near a centuries-old kapok tree under which I imagine Park once took shade. I open my bag, spread out my little red kayak, and start to pump it up. A couple of women nearby, with colorful cloth wraps called *pagnes* tied tightly about their breasts, gaze at me cryptically, as if to ask: *Who are you and what do you think you're doing?* The Niger churns and slaps the shore, in a surly mood. I don't pretend to know what I'm doing. Just one thing at a time now, kayak inflated, kayak loaded with my gear. Paddles fitted together and ready. Modibo is standing on the shore, watching me.

"I'll pray for you," he reminds me.

I balance my gear, adjust the straps, get in. And, finally, irrevocably, I paddle away.

When Mungo Park left on his second trip, he never admitted that he was scared. It is what fascinates me about his writing – his insistence on maintaining an illusion that all was well, even as he began a journey that he knew from previous experience could only beget tragedy. Hostile peoples, unknown rapids, malarial fevers. Hippos and crocodiles. The giant Lake Debo to cross, like being set adrift on an inland sea, no sight of land, no way of knowing where the river starts again. Forty of his forty-four men dead from sickness, Park himself afflicted with dysentery when he left on this ill-fated trip. And it can boggle the mind, what drives some people to risk their lives for the mute promises of success. It boggles my mind, at least, as I am caught up in the same affliction. Already, I fear the irrationality of my journey. I fear the very stubbornness which drives me forward.

The Niger erupts in a new storm. Torrential rains. Waves higher than my kayak, trying to capsize me. But my boat is self-bailing and I stay afloat. The wind drives the current in reverse, tearing and ripping at the shores, sending spray into my face. I paddle madly, crashing and driving forward. I travel inch by inch, or so it seems, arm muscles smarting and rebelling against this journey.

A popping feeling now and a screech of pain. My right

arm lurches from a ripped muscle. But this is no time and place for such an injury, and I won't tolerate it, stuck as I am in a storm. I try to get used to the metronome-like pulses of pain as I fight the river. There is only one direction to go: forward.

adobe a building material made from earth

Extract from letter to *The Times* newspaper about space exploration

> The 1950s saw the dawn of the space race, where the USA and the Soviet Union competed to explore space using satellites and manned spacecraft. The following letter was published in *The Times* newspaper on 6 January 1956 and in it the writer expresses his views on the prospect of interplanetary travel.

Sir,

I am surprised that, according to your report of January 3, our new Astronomer Royal has stated that the prospect of interplanetary travel is 'utter bilge,' although he apparently admits both that it is technically possible and that he has no idea how much it would cost.

Surely it is unwise for him to prophesy that nobody will ever put up enough money to do such a thing, when he himself can exert little or no influence on the persons who seem most likely to have to decide whether or not to finance the first expedition – namely, the next two or three Presidents of the United States, or the corresponding wielders of power in the Kremlin? While it is obvious that the next war could not be won by the first man – or even the first regiment – getting to the moon, the cold war might be decisively influenced. The propaganda value is obvious: a landing on the moon would unquestionably be man's greatest material achievement, and would no doubt be claimed to demonstrate its technical superiority to the nation concerned. It is hardly necessary for the expedition to be a financial success, any more than it is for the present Trans-Antarctic Expedition.

There are many fields of human endeavour which are more worthy of support – cancer research is an example which springs immediately to one's mind. Nevertheless we cannot confine our activities to one or two narrow branches of knowledge. We now seem to be approaching the stage at which we both need to colonize the other planets (where suitable) and have the means to do so. When the moment of history arrives no doubt some organization will be prepared to play the part of Queen Isabella. Perhaps the real question facing us in this country so far as space travel is concerned is for us to decide whether we are content that it should come about under the spur of national rivalry or whether to press for its being undertaken under the aegis of the United Nations.

I am, Sir, &c.,

G. V. E. THOMPSON

Extract from *A Fall of Moondust* by Arthur C. Clarke

Even as Yuri Gagarin became the first man in space, science fiction writers were imagining how humanity might one day travel to the Moon. The following extract is taken from the novel *A Fall of Moondust*, which was first published in 1961, and describes how the Moon has been colonized in the 21st century.

To be the skipper of the only boat on the Moon was a distinction that Pat Harris enjoyed. As the passengers filed aboard **Selene**, jockeying for window seats, he wondered what sort of trip it would be this time. In the rear-view mirror he could see Miss Wilkins, very smart in her blue Lunar Tourist Commission uniform, putting on her usual welcome act. He always tried to think of her as "Miss Wilkins," not Sue, when they were on duty together; it helped to keep his mind on business. But what she thought of him, he had never really discovered.

There were no familiar faces; this was a new bunch, eager for their first cruise. Most of the passengers were typical tourists – elderly people, visiting a world that had been the very symbol of inaccessibility when they were young. There were only four or five passengers on the low side of thirty, and they were probably technical personnel on vacation from one of the lunar bases. It was a fairly good working rule, Pat had discovered, that all the old people came from Earth, while the youngsters were residents of the Moon.

But to all of them, the **Sea of Thirst** was a novelty. Beyond Selene's observation windows, its gray, dusty surface marched onward unbroken until it reached the stars. Above it hung the waning crescent Earth, poised forever in the sky from which it had not moved in a billion years. The brilliant, blue-green light of the mother world flooded this strange land with a cold radiance – and cold it was indeed, perhaps three hundred below zero on the exposed surface.

No one could have told, merely by looking at it, whether the Sea was liquid or solid. It was completely flat and featureless, quite free from the myriad cracks and fissures that scarred all the rest of this barren world. Not a single hillock, boulder, or pebble broke its monotonous uniformity. No sea on Earth – no millpond, even – was ever as calm as this.

It was a sea of dust, not of water, and therefore it was alien to all the experience of men; therefore, also, it fascinated and attracted them. Fine as talcum powder, drier in this vacuum than the parched sands of the Sahara, it flowed as easily and effortlessly as any liquid. A heavy object dropped into it would disappear instantly, without a splash, leaving no scar to mark its passage. Nothing could move upon its treacherous surface except the small, two-man dust-skis – and Selene herself, an improbable combination of sledge and bus, not unlike the **Sno-cats** that had opened up the Antarctic a lifetime ago.

Selene's official designation was Dust-Cruiser, Mark I, though to the best of Pat's knowledge, a Mark II did not exist even on the drawing board. She was called "ship," "boat," or "moon bus," according to taste; Pat preferred "boat," for it prevented confusion. When he used that word, no one would mistake him for the skipper of a spaceship - and spaceship captains were, of course, two a penny.

"Welcome aboard Selene," said Miss Wilkins, when everyone had settled down. "Captain Hams and I are pleased to have you with us. Our trip will last four hours, and our first objective will be Crater Lake, a hundred kilometres east of here, in the Mountains of Inaccessibility.

Pat scarcely heard the familiar introduction; he was busy with his count-down. Selene was virtually a grounded spaceship; she had to be, since she was travelling in a vacuum, and must protect her frail cargo from the hostile world beyond her walls. Though she never left the surface of the Moon, and was propelled by electric motors instead of rockets, she carried all the basic equipment of a full-fledged ship of space – and all of it had to be checked before departure.

Oxygen - O. K. Power - O. K. Radio - O. K. ("Hello, Rainbow Base, Selene testing. Are you receiving my beacon?") Inertial navigator - zeroed. Air-lock safety - On. Cabin-leak detector - O. K. Internal lights - O. K. Gangway - disconnected. And so on for more than fifty items, every one of which would automatically call attention to itself in case of trouble. But Pat Harris, like all spacemen hankering after old age, never relied on auto-warnings if he could carry out the check himself.

At last he was ready. The almost silent motors started to spin, but the blades were still feathered, and Selene barely quivered at her moorings. Then he eased the port fan into fine pitch, and she began to curve slowly to the right. When she was clear of the **embarkation** building, he straightened her out and pushed the throttle forward.

She handled very well, when one considered the complete novelty of her design. There had been no millennia of trial and error here, stretching back to the first neolithic man who ever launched a log out into a stream. Selene was the very first of her line, created in the brains of a few engineers who had sat down at a table and asked themselves: "How do we build a vehicle that will skim over a sea of dust?"

Some of them, harking back to Ole Man River, had wanted to make her a stern-wheeler, but the more efficient submerged fans had carried the day. As they drilled through the dust, driving her before them, they produced a wake like that of a high-speed mole, but it vanished within seconds, leaving the Sea unmarked by any sign of the boat's passage.

Now the squat pressure-domes of Port Roris were dropping swiftly below the sky line. In less than ten minutes, they had vanished from sight: Selene was utterly alone. She was at the centre of something for which the languages of mankind have no name.

As Pat switched off the motors and the boat coasted to rest, he waited for the silence to grow around him. It was always the same; it took a little while for the passengers to realize the strangeness of what lay outside. They had crossed space and seen stars all about them; they had looked up – or down – at the dazzling face of Earth, but this was different. It was neither land nor sea, neither air nor space, but a little of each.

Selene the name of the vehicle used to travel across the moon's surface
Sea of Thirst one of the lunar seas filled with an extremely fine dust
Sno-cats a tracked vehicle used to explore snowy terrain
embarkation the process of boarding a vehicle

Accounts from the first men on the Moon

On 21 July 1969, the American astronauts Neil Armstrong and Edwin 'Buzz' Aldrin became the first humans to set foot on the surface of the Moon. The following extract is taken from their account of the mission.

NEIL ARMSTRONG: The most dramatic recollections I had were the sights themselves. Of all the spectacular views we had, the most impressive to me was on the way to the Moon, when we flew through its shadow. We were still thousands of miles away, but close enough, so that the Moon almost filled our circular window. It was eclipsing the Sun, from our position, and the corona of the Sun was visible around the limb of the Moon as a gigantic lens-shaped or saucer-shaped light, stretching out to several lunar diameters. It was magnificent, but the Moon was even more so. We were in its shadow, so there was no part of it illuminated by the Sun. It was illuminated only by earthshine. It made the Moon appear blue-grey, and the entire scene looked decidedly three-dimensional.

I was really aware, visually aware, that the Moon was

in fact a sphere not a disc. It seemed almost as if it were showing us its roundness, its similarity in shape to our Earth, in a sort of welcome. I was sure that it would be a hospitable host. It had been awaiting its first visitors for a long time . . .

[*After touchdown*] The sky is black, you know. It's a very dark sky. But it still seemed more like daylight than darkness as we looked out the window. It's a peculiar thing, but the surface looked very warm and inviting. It was the sort of situation in which you felt like going out there in nothing but a swimming suit to get a little sun. From the cockpit, the surface seemed to be tan. It's hard to account for that, because later when I held this material in my hand, it wasn't tan at all. It was black, grey and so on. It's some kind of lighting effect, but out the window the surface looks much more light desert sand than black sand . . .

EDWIN E. ALDRIN [*on the moon*]: The blue colour of my boot has completely disappeared now into this – still don't know exactly what colour to describe this other than greyish-cocoa colour. It appears to be covering most of the lighter part of my boot . . . very fine particles . . .

[*Later*] The Moon was a very natural and pleasant environment in which to work. It had many of the advantages of zero gravity, but it was in a sense less *lonesome* than Zero G, where you always have to pay attention to securing attachment points to give you some means of leverage. In one-sixth gravity, on the Moon, you had a distinct feeling of being *somewhere* . . . As we deployed our experiments on the surface we had to jettison things like lanyards, retaining fasteners, etc., and some of these we tossed away. The objects would go away with a slow, lazy motion. If anyone tried to throw a baseball back and forth in that atmosphere he would have difficulty, at first, acclimatizing himself to that slow, lazy trajectory; but I believe he could adapt to it quite readily . . .

Odour is very subjective, but to me there was a distinct smell to the lunar material – pungent like gunpowder or spent cap-pistol caps. We carted a fair amount of lunar dust back inside the vehicle with us, either on our suits and boots or on the conveyor system we used to get boxes and equipment back inside. We did notice the odour right away.

Extract from *Railhead*
by Philip Reeve

The following extract is taken from *Railhead*, a novel which was first published in 2015, which describes a future where intelligent trains travel between the stars. Here, Zen, a young petty thief, is trying to escape from a drone that is following him and enters Ambersai station where the trains depart for other planets.

Ambersai station: grand and high-fronted like a great theatre, with the K-bahn logo hanging over its entrance in letters of blue fire. Booming loudspeaker voices reciting **litanies** of stations. Moths and Monk bugs swarming under the lamps outside; beggars and street kids too, and buskers, and vendors selling fruit and chai and noodles, and rickshaw captains squabbling as they touted for fares. Through the din and the chatter came the sound of the train.

Zen went through the entrance barriers and ran out onto the platform. The Express was just pulling in. First the huge loco, a Helden Hammerhead, its long hull sheathed in shining red-gold scales. Then a line of lit windows, and a pair of station angels flickering along the carriage sides like stray rainbows. Some tourists standing next to Zen pointed at them and snapped pictures which wouldn't come out. Zen kept his place in the scrum of other K-bahn travellers, itching to look behind him, but knowing that he mustn't because, if the drone was there, it would be watching for just that: a face turned back, a look of guilt.

The doors slid open. He shoved past **disembarking** passengers into a carriage. It smelled of something sweet, as if the train had come from some world where it was springtime. Zen found a window seat and sat there looking at his feet, at the ceramic floor, at the patterns on the worn seat coverings, anywhere but out of the window, which was where he most wanted to look. His fellow passengers were commuters and a few Motorik couriers with their android brains stuffed full of information for businesses further down the line. In the seats opposite Zen lounged a couple of rich kids: railheads from K'mbussi or Galaghast, pretty as threedie stars, dozing with their arms around each other. Zen thought about taking their bags with him when he got off, but his luck was glitchy tonight and he decided not to risk it.

The train began to move, so smoothly he barely noticed. Then the lights of Ambersai Station were falling behind, the throb of the engines was rising, the backbeat of the wheels quickening. Zen risked a glance at the window. At first it was hard to make out anything in the confusion of carriage reflections and the city lights sliding by outside.

Then he saw the drone again. It was keeping pace with the train, shards of light sliding from its rotor blades as it burred along at window height, aiming a whole spider-cluster of eyes and cameras and who-knew-what at him.

The train rushed into a tunnel, and he could see nothing any more except his own skinny reflection, wide cheekbones fluttering with the movement of the carriage, eyes big and empty as the eyes on moths' wings.

The train accelerated. The noise rising, rising, until, with a soundless bang – a kind of *un-bang* – it tore through the K-gate, and everything got reassuringly weird. For a timeless moment Zen was outside of the universe. There was a sense of falling, although there was no longer any down to fall to. Something that was not quite light blazed in through the blank windows . . .

Then another un-bang, and the train was sliding out of another ordinary tunnel, slowing towards another everyday station. It was bright daytime on this world, and the gravity was lower. Zen relaxed into his seat, grinning. He was imagining that drone turning away in defeat from the empty tunnel on Ambersai, a thousand light years away.

---

litanies lists
disembarking getting off a vehicle

War and disaster

The 20th and 21st centuries have been an era scarred by war. From the outbreak of the First World War in 1914, not a year has passed without British forces being engaged in fighting somewhere in the world. From two World Wars that tore the globe apart, causing tens of millions of deaths, to more recent conflicts in Afghanistan and Iraq, the bomb and the gun have cast a long shadow over the lives of the generations who have lived through this period in history.

As well as the destruction caused by these conflicts, the world has been shaken by many disasters too, both natural and man-made. From earthquakes and tsunamis to plane crashes and sinkings, these cataclysmic events have left grief and havoc in their wake. And as humanity's knowledge has grown, we are now increasingly aware of potential disasters to come, from the threat of climate change to world-ending catastrophes such as a meteor strike from outer space.

Extract from *Some Desperate Glory: The World War I Diary of a British Officer* by Edwin Campion Vaughan

> The following extract is taken from a diary written by a British army officer, Edwin Campion Vaughan, during the First World War, but first published in 1981. Here, he describes coming under fire as he leads an attack on an enemy position.

Immediately there came the crackle of bullets and mud was spattered about me as I ran, crawled and dived into shell-holes, over bodies, sometimes up to the armpits in water, sometimes crawling on my face along a ridge of slimy mud around some crater . . . As I neared the gunpits I saw a head rise above a shell-hole, a mouth opened to call something to me, but the tin hat was sent flying and the face fell forward into the mud . . .

I had almost reached the gunpits when I saw Wood looking at me, and actually laughing at my grotesque capers. Exhausted by my efforts, I paused a moment in a shell-hole; in a few seconds I felt myself sinking, and struggle as I might I was sucked down until I was firmly gripped round the waist and still being dragged in. The leg of a corpse was sticking out of the side, and frantically I grabbed it; it wrenched off and casting it down I pulled in a couple of rifles and yelled to the troops in the gunpit to throw me more. Laying them flat I wriggled over them and dropped, half dead, into the wrecked gun position.

Here I reported to Taylor and was filled with admiration at the calm way in which he stood, eyeglass firmly fixed in his ashen face, while bullets chipped splinters from the beam beside his head. He told me that the attack had not even reached the enemy front line, and that it was impossible to advance across the mud. Then he ordered me to take my company up the hard road to the Triangle and to attack Springfield. He gave his instructions in such a matter-of-fact way that I did not feel alarmed, but commenced forthwith to collect "C" Company men from the neighbouring shell-holes . . .

So many of our men had been killed, and the rest had gone to ground so well, that Wood and I could only collect a very few . . . Finally, Wood and I led 15 men over to the tanks. The fire was still heavy, but now, in the dusk and heavy rain, the shots were going wide. As we reached the tanks, however, the **Boche** hailed shrapnel upon us and we commenced rapidly to have casualties . . . Up the road we staggered, shells bursting around us. A man stopped dead in front of me, and exasperated I cursed him and butted him with my knee. Very gently he said,

"I'm blind, sir," and turned to show me his eyes and nose torn away by a piece of shell.

"Oh God! I'm sorry, sonny," I said. "Keep going on the hard part," and left him staggering back in his darkness. At the Triangle the shelling was lighter and the rifle fire far above our heads. Around us were numerous dead, and in shell-holes where they had crawled to safety were wounded men. Many others, too weak to move, were lying where they had fallen and they cheered us faintly as we passed: "Go on boys! Give 'em hell!" . . .

A tank had churned its way slowly round behind Springfield and opened fire; a moment later I looked and nothing remained of it but a crumpled heap of iron; it had been hit by a large shell. It was now almost dark and there was no firing from the enemy; ploughing across the final stretch of mud, I saw grenades bursting around the **pillbox** and a party of British rushed in from the other side. As we all closed in, the Boche garrison ran out with their hands up; in the confused party I recognised Reynolds of the 7th Battalion, who had been working forward all the afternoon. We sent the 16 prisoners back across the open but they had only gone 100 yards when a German machine-gun mowed them down.

Reynolds and I held a rapid conference and decided that the cemetery and Spot Farm were far too strongly held for us to attack, especially as it was then quite dark; so we formed a line with my party on the left in touch

228

with the Worcesters, who had advanced some 300 yards further than we, and Reynolds formed a flank guard back to the line where our attack had broken. I entered Springfield, which was to be my HQ. It was a strongly built pillbox, almost undamaged; the three defence walls were about 10ft thick, each with a machine-gun position, while the fourth wall, which faced our new line, had one small doorway – about 3ft square. Crawling through this I found the interior in a horrible condition; water in which floated indescribable filth reached our knees; two dead Boche sprawled face downwards and another lay across a wire bed. Everywhere was dirt and rubbish and the stench was nauseating.

Boche a derogatory term used to refer to German soldiers during the First World War
pillbox guard post

Extract from *Good-Bye to All That* by Robert Graves

The following extract is taken from the autobiography of the writer, Robert Graves, which was first published in 1929. Here, he describes his experiences serving as a British army officer in the First World War.

The roadside cottages were now showing more and more signs of **dilapidation**. A German shell came over and then whoo - oo - oooooooOOO - bump - CRASH! twenty yards away from the party. We threw ourselves flat on our faces. Presently we heard a curious singing noise in the air, and then flop! flop! little pieces of shell-casing came buzzing down all around. 'They calls them the musical instruments,' said the sergeant. 'Damn them,' said Frank Jones-Bateman, who had a cut in his hand from a jagged little piece, 'the devils have started on me early.' 'Aye, they'll have a lot of fun with you before they're done, sir,' grinned the sergeant. Another shell came over. Every one threw himself down again, but it burst two hundred yards behind us. Only Sergeant Jones had remained on his feet and laughed at us. 'You're wasting yourselves, lads,' he said to the draft. 'Listen by the noise they make coming where they're going to burst.'

At Cambrin village, about a mile from the front trenches, we were taken into a ruined chemist's shop with its coloured glass jars still in the window: the **billet** of the four Welsh company-quartermaster-sergeants. Here they gave us respirators and field-dressings. This, the first respirator issued in France, was a gauze-pad filled with chemically treated cotton waste, for tying across the mouth and nose. Reputedly it could not keep out the German gas, which had been used at Ypres against the Canadian Division; but we never put it to the test. A week or two later came the 'smoke-helmet', a greasy grey-felt bag with a talc window to look through, and no mouth-piece, certainly ineffective against gas. The talc was always cracking, and visible leaks showed at the stitches joining it to the helmet.

These were early days of trench warfare, the days of the jam-tin bomb and the gas-pipe trench mortar: still innocent of Lewis or Stokes guns, steel helmets, telescopic rifle-sights, gas-shells, pill-boxes, tanks, well-organized trench raids, or any of the later refinements of trench warfare.

After a meal of bread, bacon, rum, and bitter stewed tea sickly with sugar, we went through the broken trees to the east of the village and up a long trench to battalion headquarters. The wet and slippery trench ran through dull red clay. I had a torch with me, and saw that hundreds of field mice and frogs had fallen into the trench but found no way out. The light dazzled them, and because I could not help treading on them, I put the torch back in my pocket. We had no mental picture of what the trenches would be like, and were almost as ignorant as a young soldier who joined us a week or two later. He called out excitedly to old Burford, who was cooking up a bit of stew in a **dixie**, apart from the others: 'Hi, mate, where's the battle? I want to do my bit.'

The guide gave us hoarse directions all the time. 'Hole right' 'Wire high.' 'Wire low.' 'Deep place here, sir.' 'Wire low.' The field-telephone wires had been fastened by staples to the side of the trench, and when it rained the staples were constantly falling out and the wire falling down and tripping people up. If it sagged too much, one stretched it across the trench to the other side to correct the sag, but then it would catch one's head. The holes were sump-pits used for draining the trenches.

We now came under rifle-fire, which I found more trying than shell-fire. The gunner, I knew, fired not at people but at map references – crossroads, likely artillery positions, houses that suggested billets for troops, and so on. Even when an observation officer in an aeroplane or captive balloon, or on a church spire directed the guns, it seemed random, somehow. But a rifle-bullet, even when fired blindly, always seemed purposely aimed. And whereas we could usually hear a shell approaching, and take some sort of cover, the rifle-bullet gave no warning. So, though we learned not to duck a rifle-bullet because, once heard, it must have missed, it gave us a worse feeling of danger. Rifle-bullets in the open went hissing into the grass without much noise, but when we were in a trench, the bullets made a tremendous crack as they went over the hollow. Bullets often struck the barbed wire in front of the trenches, which sent them spinning with a head-over-heels motion – ping! rockety-ockety-ockety-ockety into the woods behind.

---

dilapidation falling to pieces
billet a temporary lodging for soldiers
dixie a large metal pot used for cooking

233

Extract from a speech by Winston Churchill

> The following extract is taken from a speech given by Winston Churchill to the House of Commons on 4 June 1940. Here, the British Prime Minister warns of a possible invasion attempt by Nazi Germany.

I have, myself, full confidence that if all do their duty, if nothing is neglected, and if the best arrangements are made, as they are being made, we shall prove ourselves once again able to defend our Island home, to ride out the storm of war, and to outlive the menace of tyranny, if necessary for years, if necessary alone.

At any rate, that is what we are going to try to do. That is the resolve of His Majesty's Government – every man of them. That is the will of Parliament and the nation.

The British Empire and the French Republic, linked together in their cause and in their need, will defend to the death their native soil, aiding each other like good comrades to the utmost of their strength.

Even though large tracts of Europe and many old and famous States have fallen or may fall into the grip of the

Gestapo and all the odious apparatus of Nazi rule, we shall not flag or fail.

We shall go on to the end, we shall fight in France, we shall fight on the seas and oceans, we shall fight with growing confidence and growing strength in the air, we shall defend our Island, whatever the cost may be, we shall fight on the beaches, we shall fight on the landing grounds, we shall fight in the fields and in the streets, we shall fight in the hills; we shall never surrender, and even if, which I do not for a moment believe, this Island or a large part of it were **subjugated** and starving, then our Empire beyond the seas, armed and guarded by the British Fleet, would carry on the struggle, until, in God's good time, the New World, with all its power and might, steps forth to the rescue and the liberation of the old.

subjugated conquered

Extract from *A Piece of Cake* by Roald Dahl

> The following extract is taken from Roald Dahl's short story 'A Piece of Cake' which takes place during the Second World War. Here, a pilot is flying his plane low over the Libyan desert as he searches for his destination.

I know only that there was trouble, lots and lots of trouble, and I know that we had turned round and were coming back when the trouble got worse. The biggest trouble of all was that I was too low to bail out, and it is from that point on that my memory comes back to me. I remember the dipping of the nose of the aircraft and I remember looking down the nose of the machine at the ground and seeing a little clump of camel-thorn growing there all by itself. I remember seeing some rocks lying in the sand beside the camel-thorn, and the camel-thorn and the sand and the rocks leapt out of the ground and came to me. I remember that very clearly.

Then there was a small gap of not-remembering. It might have been one second or it might have been thirty; I do not know. I have an idea that it was very short, a second perhaps, and next I heard a *crumph* on the left as the port tank did the same. To me that was not significant, and for a while I sat still, feeling comfortable, but a little drowsy. I couldn't see with my eyes, but that was not significant either. There was nothing to worry about. Nothing at all. Not until I felt the hotness around my legs. At first it was only a warmness and that was all right too, but all at once it was a hotness, a very stinging scorching hotness up and down the sides of each leg.

I knew that the hotness was unpleasant, but that was all I knew. I disliked it, so I curled my legs up under the seat and waited. I think there was something wrong with the telegraph system between the body and the brain. It did not seem to be working very well. Somehow it was a bit slow in telling the brain all about it and in asking for instructions. But I believe a message eventually got through, saying, 'Down here there is a great hotness. What shall we do? (Signed) Left Leg and Right Leg.' For a long time there was no reply. The brain was figuring the matter out.

Then slowly, word by word, the answer was tapped over the wires. 'The – plane – is – burning. Get – out – repeat – get – out – get – out.' The order was relayed to the whole system, to all the muscles in the legs, arms and body, and the muscles went to work. They tried their best; they pushed a little and pulled a little, and they strained greatly, but it wasn't any good. Up went another telegram. 'Can't get out. Something holding us

237

in.' The answer to this one took even longer in arriving, so I just sat there waiting for it to come, and all the time the hotness increased. Something was holding me down and it was up to the brain to find out what it was. Was it giants' hands pressing on my shoulders, or heavy stones or houses or steam rollers or filing cabinets or gravity or was it ropes? Wait a minute. Ropes – ropes. The message was beginning to come through. It came very slowly. 'Your – straps. Undo – your – straps.' My arms received the message and went to work. They tugged at the straps, but they wouldn't undo. They tugged again and again, a little feebly, but as hard as they could, and it wasn't any use. Back went the message, 'How do we undo the straps?'

This time I think that I sat there for three or four minutes waiting for the answer. It wasn't any use hurrying or getting impatient. That was the one thing of which I was sure. But what a long time it was all taking. I said aloud, 'Bugger it. I'm going to be burnt. I'm . . .' but I was interrupted. The answer was coming – no, it wasn't – yes, it was, it was slowly coming through, 'Pull – out – the – quick – release – pin – you – bloody – fool – and – hurry.'

Out came the pin and the straps were loosed. Now, let's get out. Let's get out, let's get out. But I couldn't do it. I simply lift myself out of the cockpit. Arms and legs tried their best but it wasn't any use. A last desperate message was flashed upwards and this time it was marked 'Urgent'.

'Something else is holding us down,' it said. 'Something else, something else, something heavy.'

Still the arms and legs did not fight. They seemed to know instinctively that there was no point in using up their strength. They stayed quiet and waited for the answer, and oh what a time it took. Twenty, thirty, forty hot seconds. None of them really white hot yet, no sizzling of flesh or smell of burning meat, but that would come any moment now, because those old **Gladiators** aren't made of stressed steel like a **Hurricane** or a **Spit**. They have taut canvas wings, covered with magnificently inflammable dope, and underneath there are hundreds of small thin sticks, the kind you put under the logs for kindling, only these are drier and thinner. If a clever man said, 'I am going to build a big thing that will burn better and quicker than anything else in the world,' and if he applied himself diligently to his task, he would probably finish up by building something very like a Gladiator. I sat still waiting.

Then suddenly the reply, beautiful in its briefness, but at the same time explaining everything. 'Your – parachute – turn – the – buckle.'

I turned the buckle, released the parachute harness and with some effort hoisted myself up and tumbled over the side of the cockpit. Something seemed to be burning, so I rolled about a bit in the sand, then crawled away from the fire on all fours and lay down.

I heard some of my machine-gun ammunition going off in the heat and I heard some of the bullets thumping into the sand near by. I did not worry about them; I merely heard them.

Things were beginning to hurt.

Gladiator a biplane
Hurricane a fighter aircraft
Spit spitfire, a fighter aircraft

Extract from a survivor's account of the sinking of *The Titanic*

> The *Titanic* was a passenger liner which sank in the Atlantic Ocean on 15 April 1912 after colliding with an iceberg. Here, a fireman named Harry Senior describes his experiences on the night the ship sank.

I was in my bunk when I felt a bump. One man said, "Hello! She has been struck." I went on deck and saw a great pile of ice on the well deck before the **forecastle**, but we all thought the ship would last some time, and we went back to our bunks. Then one of the firemen came running down and yelled, "All muster for the lifeboats." I ran on deck, and the Captain said, "All firemen keep down on the well deck. If a man comes up I'll shoot him."

Then I saw the first lifeboat lowered. Thirteen people were on board, eleven men and two women. Three were millionaires and one was **Ismay**.

Then I ran up on to the hurricane deck and helped to throw one of the collapsible boats on to the lower deck. I saw an Italian woman holding two babies. I took one of them, and made the woman jump overboard with the baby, while I did the same with the other. When I came to the surface the baby in my arms was dead. I saw the woman strike out in good style, but a boiler burst on the Titanic and started a big wave. When the woman saw that wave, she gave up. Then, as the child was dead, I let it sink too.

I swam around for about half an hour, and was swimming on my back when the Titanic went down. I tried to get aboard a boat, but some chap hit me over the head with an oar. There were too many in her. I got around to the other side of the boat and climbed in.

---

forecastle upper deck
Ismay J. Bruce Ismay, the Managing Director of the company which owned the *Titanic*

Extract from *Every Man For Himself* by Beryl Bainbridge

FICTION

> The sinking of the *Titanic* has inspired novels, films and poetry. The following extract is taken from the novel *Every Man For Himself*, which was first published in 1996. Here, the narrator describes the moment the ship sank.

At that moment the orchestra changed tune and struck up a hymn, one I knew well because it was a favourite of my aunt's and sometimes she used to sing it when she was in one of her brighter moods . . . *E'en though it be a cross that raiseth me, Still all my song shall be, Nearer my God to Thee, Nearer to Thee.* Hearing it, I knew I had to go in search of Charlie, for Lady Melchett's sake if not my own, and would have gone on searching for him if Scurra hadn't been waiting for me at the bottom of the steps. He said, 'A man bears the weight of his own body without knowing it, but he soon feels the weight of any other object. There is nothing, absolutely nothing, that a man cannot forget – but not himself.' Then, before walking away, he said those other things, about it being the drop, not the height, that was terrible, and I left Charlie to God and went back up to the officers' house.

And now, the moment was almost upon us. The stern began to lift from the water. Guggenheim and his valet played mountaineers, going hand over hand up the rail. The hymn turned ragged; ceased altogether. The musicians scrambled upwards, the spike of the cello scraping the deck. Clinging to the rung of the ladder I tried to climb to the roof but there was such a sideways slant that I waved like a flag on a pole. I thought I must make a leap for it and turned to look for Hopper. Something, some inner voice urged me to glance below and I saw Scurra again, one arm hooked through the rail to steady himself. I raised my hand in greeting – then the water, first slithering, then tumbling, gushed us apart.

As the ship staggered and tipped, a great volume of water flowed in over the submerged bows and tossed me like a cork to the roof. Hopper was there too. My fingers touched some kind of bolt near the ventilation grille and I grabbed it tight. I filled my lungs with air and fixed my eyes on the blurred horizon, determined to hang on until I was sure I could float free rather than be swilled back and forth in a maelstrom. I wouldn't waste my strength in swimming, not yet, for I knew the ship was now my enemy and if I wasn't vigilant would drag me with her to the grave. I waited for the next slithering dip and when it came and the waves rushed in and swept me higher, I released my grip and let myself be carried away, over the tangle of ropes and wires and davits, clear of the rails and out into the darkness. I heard the angry roaring of the dying ship, the deafening cacophony as she stood on end and all her guts tore loose. I choked on soot and cringed beneath the sparks dancing like fire-flies as the forward funnel broke and smashed the sea in two. I thought I saw Hopper's face but one eye was ripped away and he gobbled like a fish on the hook. I was sucked under, as I knew I would be, down, down, and still I waited, waited until the pull slackened – then I struck out with all my strength.

I don't know how long I swam under that lidded sea – time had stopped with my breath – and just as it seemed as if my lungs would burst the blackness paled and I kicked to the surface. I had thought I was entering paradise, for I was alive and about to breathe again, and then I heard the cries of souls in torment and believed myself in hell. Dear God! Those voices! *Father . . . Father . . . For the love of Christ . . . Help me, for pity's sake! . . . Where is my son.* Some called for their mothers, some on the Lord, some to die quickly, a few to be saved. The **lamentations** rang through the frosty air and touched the stars; my own mouth opened in a silent howl of grief. The cries went on and on, trembling, lingering – and God forgive me, but I wanted them to end. In all that ghastly night it was the din of the dying that chilled the most. Presently, the voices grew fainter, ceased – yet still I heard them, as though the drowned called to one another in a ghostly place where none could follow. Then silence fell, and that was the worst sound of all. There was no trace of the *Titanic*. All that remained was a grey veil of vapour drifting above the water.

---

lamentations expressions of grief

Extract from a magazine article from *The Guardian* newspaper

NON-FICTION

On Boxing Day in 2004, an earthquake struck beneath the Indian Ocean, triggering a tsunami that killed more than 230,000 people in fourteen countries. The following extract is taken from a magazine article published in *The Guardian* newspaper on 15 November 2014 and describes the experience of Edie Fassnidge who lost both her mother and sister in the tsunami.

'Surviving the tsunami'

Just before the first wave hit, Edie Fassnidge took a picture of her younger sister Alice and their mother. The scene was idyllic, Boxing Day 2004, the three of them kayaking off Ao Nang beach in Thailand with Fassnidge's boyfriend, Matt: blue skies, clear waters, perfectly calm weather. "I remember saying, 'It's so beautiful here,'" Fassnidge says. "We were floating along in the sea, and there was a dramatic limestone column right by us, a little island in the background, and we were all really happy."

The camera was still aloft when something in the air shifted. Fassnidge's mood switched to high alert. "I caught sight of the horizon and suddenly that didn't look right. Everything had been so calm and now there was a ridge all the way along it." A wave was approaching them – her mother and Alice in one kayak, she and Matt in the other. They were a kilometre from the nearest beach, but only a few metres from a rocky, vertical cliff. "My mind was going crazy, trying to make sense of what I was seeing."

Fassnidge noticed her mother and Alice paddling towards the rocks and shouted at them to stop, before water engulfed them all. She was pulled from her boat, into a bank of rocks, her head pounding against them, over and over. Her mother and sister were swept away.

Then the waves came. After that first one, Fassnidge tumbled underwater until everything calmed around her. When she regained some control of her body, she kicked up and found she was trapped beneath a wall of solid rock; as she felt her way along, she started panicking, deeply aware of her lack of oxygen. Finally, her hand reached into clear water and she rose up through the blue.

At the surface, she saw Matt, Alice and her mother a few metres away, all treading water. "I was so happy – so, so happy – and I was about to say to everyone, 'It's all fine!' when I realised they didn't look fine, any of them. They all looked very, very distant, just staring, not saying anything." A couple of seconds later she watched, appalled, as another wave rose behind them.

She was pulled under again, and emerged to find her family had disappeared. As she swam around looking for some sign of them, another wave hit, and when she broke the surface for the third time, she saw her mother's body five metres away in the water. "I swam over to her and she was face down. I turned her over and knew she was dead, but I wanted to see if I could bring her back to life, so I breathed into her mouth. I had hold of her, and my back to the sea, but I sensed something else." Another wave. "I knew my mum was dead and that if I stayed in the water, I could die, too."

Fassnidge swam to some nearby rocks, pulled herself out and scrambled as high as she could, holding on to rushes as the waves crashed around her. "When the water died down, I looked to see whether my mum was there, and her body had gone. Then I looked down at myself and I was speechless. I couldn't feel any pain, but where the rocks had torn me, I was covered everywhere with lacerations and cuts. It was the strangest experience, because I thought that when people looked like I looked, they screamed, but I was just completely numb."

Alone on the rocks, she considered her chances of being rescued. At that stage, she had no idea of the scale of what had just happened – she assumed the tsunami had just been a freak, local wave and that a search party would be along soon. But she also realised that she was very isolated. There was no way to dry land except via the sea, and since she was now terrified of the water, she started climbing up the rocky headland. "Before long I was climbing through really dense, spiky gorse bushes, pulling myself up through branches; I could feel myself getting cut even more. It was getting steeper and steeper, and I realised that it wasn't going to work. I needed to turn back and preserve my energy."

On climbing down, she was suddenly surrounded by large, orangey-brown ants. "I felt them first in my feet, which were really cut up; it was as if something was biting into the core of my body, electric pain, like an electric shock, and they swarmed all over me." There were too many to pick off, and this was the first time that she cried. "I got really angry and I screamed, 'Why is this happening to me?'" She moved down to the water, heard a helicopter, and motioned to it, shouting. It was flying low, but didn't slow down, just kept moving on out to sea. There was no option but to follow it, to do what she was dreading: she lowered herself back into the water.

Fassnidge swam against the currents, then rested, aware of how close she might be to dying if she didn't get help. "I was feeling drained and out of energy, out of ideas. I lay down and gave myself a bit of a talking to, told myself that if I didn't do anything, I could die." Finally she saw a small gap between some rocks and decided to squeeze through. She emerged on to a small, rocky beach. After so long without water she knew she was running solely on adrenaline, but she crawled, walked and paddled as far as she could, finally turning a corner and seeing two men next to some boats. A paramedic arrived and she was carried to a beach; she hadn't spoken for hours, but her story began tumbling out.

Extract from *In Darkness*
by Nick Lake

> The following extract from the novel *In Darkness*,
> first published in 2012, is set in the aftermath of the
> devastating earthquake that struck Haiti in 2010. Here,
> fifteen-year-old Shorty has been buried alive in the pitch-
> black rubble of the hospital where he was being treated.

Sometime today or another day, I heard people shouting from far, far away in the darkness. It sounded like:

— . . . survived?

— . . . alive . . . in there?

— . . . wounded?

I shouted back. You can guess what I shouted. I shouted, yes. I shouted, help. I shouted those words in French and English. I shouted in **Kreyòl** to tell them there was an accident and I was hurt. Then I thought that was a dumb-ass thing to shout, cos this is a hospital, so of course I was hurt, and it must have been **anpil** obvious there had been an accident, with everything fallen down.

But nobody answered and the voices went away. I don't know when that was. I don't know when it's night and when it's day, or even if night and day exist anymore.

If I can hear people shouting, but they can't hear me, does that make me a ghost? I think, maybe yes. I can't see myself. I can't prove that I exist.

But then I think, no, I can't be a ghost. A ghost does not get thirsty, and as I'm lying here in the broken hospital it's like my mouth is bigger than me, bigger than the darkness. Like my mouth contains the world, not the other way round. It's dry and sore and I can't think of anything else. My thinking, cos of my thirst, is like this:

... WATER, WATER, WATER, WATER, WATER, WATER. Am I dead? WATER, WATER, WATER, WATER. What happened? WATER, WATER, WATER, WATER. Is this the end of the world? WATER, WATER, WATER, WATER, WATER, WATER ...

That is how my mouth swallows everything else. Maybe my mouth will swallow me, and then this will be over.

I decide to crawl, to measure the space of my prison. I know the rubble and the hand on my left – I don't need to go there again. I don't want to touch that clammy skin. In front of me, and to my right and behind me, is just darkness, though maybe I should stop calling it that cos there's no light at all; it's more blackness. I shift forward on my hands and knees, and I scream when my wrist bends a little and the wound opens. The scream echoes off the concrete all around me.

I shuffle, and I feel like I'm not a person anymore, like

I've turned into some animal. I move maybe one body length and then I hit a wall of blocks. I reach up with my hands and stand up, and I feel that it goes up to the ceiling. Only the ceiling is lower than I remember, so that's not great, either. To my right, the same thing – a broken bed, then a wall of rubble. And behind me. I'm in a space maybe one body length in each direction.

I'm in a coffin.

Kreyòl Creole, a language used in Haiti
anpil a Haitian Creole word meaning 'very'

Extract from a newspaper article in *The Guardian*

The following extract is taken from a newspaper article which was first published in *The Guardian* on 30 September 2014 and explores the threat posed to the Earth by an asteroid strike.

Asteroids: between a rock and a hard place

There have been recent near misses – an explosion over Russia, a mysterious crater in Nicaragua. But what would we do in the event of an actual meteor strike?

In February 2013, a large asteroid ripped over the Chelyabinsk district of Russia, trailing cartoonish lines of smoke as it made its shallow entry, radiating so much light and heat that onlookers were left with reddened faces. Skin peel. When the asteroid exploded, 15 miles up, there was a terrible, prolonged bang – a noise that has rung on, in its way, ever since.

We now know that the explosion over Chelyabinsk occurred with a force equal to 500 kilotons of TNT, or a couple of dozen Nagasaki bombs. Had it come down a little steeper that February, directing the might of its detonation at rather than over Chelyabinsk, the asteroid would have killed thousands on the ground. A little later, it might have done for many more in Moscow, or Riga, or Gothenburg. Though nobody died at Chelyabinsk, it was an event of such calamitous potential that the asteroid was classified by certain astronomers a "city-killer". Those astronomers have wondered, since, if we're not being a little complacent.

In November last year, having had months to chew on the data from Chelyabinsk, a Nasa scientist called Bill Cooke said the likely frequency of such meteor strikes was being re-evaluated. That month, a trio of studies published in the journals Nature and Science suggested impacts of Chelyabinsk's magnitude were between three and 10 times more likely to happen than previously supposed. The UN, in December, called for the creation of an international asteroid warning network. Come the new year, it took only hours for the first major rock of 2014 to arrive: a car-sized lump that burst apart over the Atlantic on 1 January.

To recap: asteroids are hunks of space rock that whisk around the solar system in orbits around the sun, colliding with anything that crosses their path. If they collide with Earth, we call them meteorites. Most are small and burn up in our atmosphere; some are big enough to matter, such as the Chelyabinsk rock, which was the size of a swimming pool, 20m from end to end. Though Nasa has for some time been tracking giant asteroids (those at least 1km wide), it has never seemed much concerned about lesser rocks – those capable only of scraping away a city, say.

At a press conference earlier this year, former Nasa astronaut Dr Edward Lu announced that there are around 1m asteroids in the Earth's vicinity "with the potential to destroy a major metropolitan area". He teed up an animated graphic to demonstrate how unprepared we are. The graphic showed the Earth in orbit among the dangerous asteroids we knew about and were tracking, around 10,000 of them. Seen like this, our planet looked like a pedestrian hustling along a busy street, not overly troubled. Then Lu changed the graphic to show "what it really looks like out there" – the Earth ploughing on through a million-strong field of city-killing asteroids. I saw the same pedestrian, now trying to make it across a train station concourse in the middle of rush hour, avoiding collisions purely by fluke. "Blind luck," as Lu put it.

This information, I thought, watching online, was appalling. Why wasn't it all over the nightly news? I can't be the only person who feels fidgety on the subject, having watched Deep Impact and Armageddon at an impressionable age. I watched some of the YouTube videos of the Chelyabinsk strike, dozens of them recorded on mobile phones, and found that though the images were shocking (people swept flat by the shock of the impact), it was the noise that was truly unbearable.

The meteorite's *thoom* rang on for longer than made sense; it sounded unnatural, or maybe too natural. It seemed to contain an old message. Don't get comfy, Beijing. Look alive, London.